AN ACT
OF
MERCY

AN ACT
OF
MERCY:
EUTHANASIA
TODAY

BY
RICHARD TRUBO

Nash Publishing, Los Angeles

The author and publisher wish to acknowledge separately permission to quote from the following sources:

Hodder & Stoughton, for excerpt from *The Christian Agnostic* by Leslie Weatherhead. Copyright © 1965 by Leslie Weatherhead.
Alfred A. Knopf, Inc., for excerpts from *The Sanctity of Life and the Criminal Law* by Glanville Williams. Copyright © 1957 by the Trustees of Columbia University in the City of New York.
Longmans, Green & Co., for excerpt from *The Problem of Right Conduct* by Peter Green. Copyright © 1931 by Peter Green.
The Macmillan Company, for excerpts from *On Death and Dying* by Elisabeth Kubler-Ross. Copyright © 1969 by Elisabeth Kubler-Ross. The use of passages by Dr. Kubler-Ross in this book does not imply implicitly or explicitly her agreement with any other part of the book.
The Press of Case Western Reserve University, for excerpts from *Death and Dying: Current Issues in the Treatment of the Dying Patient* by Cicely Saunders, and edited by Leonard Pearson. Copyright © 1969 by The Press of Case Western Reserve University.
Princeton University Press, for excerpts from *Morals and Medicine* by Joseph Fletcher. Copyright © 1954 by Princeton University Press.
University of Chicago Press, for excerpts from *Family Planning and Population Programs* by Dr. Alan F. Guttmacher. Copyright © 1966 by The University of Chicago.

All case histories cited herein can be substantiated,
but for obvious reasons the
identities of the persons involved have been protected.

For my parents,
who care.

Contents

AN ACT
OF
MERCY

1. Euthanasia—
an Issue
for the Seventies

We are living in an age of medical miracles. Medicine has made such dramatic progress in the past few decades that man is now capable of lifesaving feats that were unthinkable just a generation ago. Critically ill patients throughout the world are kept alive by respirators, pacemakers, defibrillators, drugs, blood transfusions, organ transplants, and artificial kidneys. Lungs that have stopped breathing are being supported by artificial machines; hearts that have stopped beating are being restarted. The leading causes of death in the early 1900s—pneumonia, tuberculosis, and influenza—have been largely restrained. It is truly a time of miracles.

But these biomedical and technical advances are having a dual effect. True, in many instances, they are prolonging life. But in many other cases, they are more accurately prolonging death. One of the major fears of modern man is that he may

3

someday face an agonizing and lingering end—withheld from a natural death for weeks, months, and even years in a state of constant discomfort and pain. Hospital wards are crowded with patients kept alive through "heroic" means long after their minds and spirits have given up. While medicine can now often delay death, in the process it sometimes makes dying slower, more painful, and more undignified than it has ever been before.

Suddenly, doctors are being confronted with monumental decisions that physicians never before had to make. For example, what treatment should be given to a patient whose lungs have been permanently paralyzed by polio, and whose brain has been incurably damaged by a deficiency of oxygen? Should he be kept alive indefinitely through intravenous feeding, a tracheotomy, and an artificial breathing machine? Or, because he has no chance for a meaningful life again, should he be allowed to die peacefully?

Questions like these are tormenting medical men, theologians, lawyers, and families of the incurably ill. Each day, doctors are being asked by relatives of the terminally sick to do "everything you can" to keep their loved ones alive; but, just as frequently, families are pleading that the suffering patient please be allowed to die. And in many instances, the sufferer is permitted to expire.

Euthanasia—the act of inducing death for merciful reasons—is often seen as the more humane alternative in a growing number of medical cases. Despite the fact that it is technically illegal in all fifty states, some doctors are now practicing it. Physicians like Dr. Walter W. Sackett of Miami have openly admitted to "letting hundreds of my patients go." Others who say they have not rendered euthanasia themselves are nevertheless asking that the controversial and

4

complex issue be discussed and debated publicly in the upcoming years.

Although it is generally a taboo subject today, euthanasia is not a new issue. The word itself originated in the seventeenth century when, according to the *Oxford English Dictionary*, euthanasia meant simply "a quiet and easy death." Since then, new interpretations have evolved, including the one offered in *Webster's New World Dictionary:* "an act or method of causing death painlessly so as to end the intractable suffering of victims of incurable disease."

But the concept of euthanasia is much older than the word itself. It was frequently practiced in ancient times. In the first century B.C., on the Greek island of Cos, elderly and ill people would assemble at an annual banquet to consume a poisonous drink. The medical historian Sigerist reports that, in many other instances, doctors directly provided their dying patients with poisons to release them from their pain. A death potion was always kept in a public place in the Greek colony of Massila, to be used by those who could convince public officials that their death was justified. Aristotle advocated euthanasia for seriously deformed children. And Cicero wrote, "What reason is there for us to suffer? A door is open for us—death, eternal refuge where one is sensible of nothing."

Seneca believed that euthanasia is preferable when death is inevitable, and that it is an alternative that should be available to all men. He wrote, "If I can choose between a death of torture and one that is simple and easy, why should I not select the latter? As I choose the ship in which I will sail, and the house I will inhabit, so I will choose the death by which I will leave life. . . . Why should I endure the agonies of disease . . . when I can emancipate myself from all my torment. . . . I will not depart by death from disease as long as it may be healed and leaves my mind unimpaired. . . . But if I know that I will suffer forever I will depart, not through fear of the pain itself but because it prevents all for which I would live."

In later times, Sir Thomas More raised the euthanasia issue. In the second book of *Utopia,* the noted Catholic wrote of the terminally ill in his ideal society, "If the disease be not only incurable, but also full of continual pain and anguish, then the priests and the magistrates exhort the man, seeing he is not able to do any duty of life, and by over-living his own death is noisome and irksome to others, and grievous to himself, that he will determine with himself no longer to cherish that pestilent and painful disease. And seeing that his life is to him but a torment, that he will not be unwilling to die, but rather . . . either dispatch himself out of that painful life as out of a prison, or a rack of torment, or else suffer himself to be rid out of it by other."

In another book about a visionary community, Francis Bacon's *New Atlantis,* the subject was again discussed. "I esteem it," wrote Bacon, "the office of a physician not only to restore the health, but to mitigate pain and dolours; and not only when such mitigation may conduce to recovery, but when it may serve to make a fair and easy passage."

Today euthanasia is being practiced discreetly in almost every hospital in the country. Its frequency, though, can only be guessed at. In a recent poll of 156 Chicago physicians (internists and surgeons), 61 percent admitted that they have at one time or another practiced some form of euthanasia, most frequently by omitting extraordinary lifesaving techniques in the treatment of hopelessly ill patients. Although this percentage is considerably higher than some other surveys have indicated, it is still valid evidence that euthanasia does occur.

Vast medical progress is forcing doctors to question the wisdom of using all medical techniques available to keep a patient alive. Heroic techniques now allow doctors to maintain some semblance of life in a patient even in the most unreasonable circumstances. Dr. Eliot Slater, one of England's most distinguished mental health specialists, says, "It is now possible to keep a dying person alive almost indefinitely, but medical tradition is such that doctors are frightened of an impairment of a patient's right to live, and accordingly, people are kept alive against all good sense."

In a 1969 speech to the Fifth International Conference for Suicide Prevention in London, Dr. Slater said that to the thoughtful person, the fears of dying and death have been overshadowed by the fear of what modern medicine may put him through in intensive care units. "There is nothing more frightening," he explained, "than spending your last days in a vegetable-like existence, mindless and incontinent."

Dr. Slater is certainly not suggesting that medicine be viewed as an enemy of the elderly and the ill. After all, medical science can rightfully take much of the credit for our increased life expectancy today. The number of people over sixty-five has been increasing at three times the growth rate of the general population. Nearly 10 percent of all Americans—about twenty million persons—are over the age of sixty-five, and about one-third of these people are past seventy-five. According to current trends, the Bureau of the Census predicts that the proportion of the population over sixty-five will soon rise to 16 percent.

However, although medicine is allowing Americans to live longer, it has not always enhanced the "quality" of that elderly life. Whereas most people once died relatively quick deaths from acute diseases, today they frequently endure long and painful chronic diseases before they pass away.

In earlier times, nature itself made many of man's life-and-

7

death decisions. For example, pneumonia was one of the commonest killers of the ill and elderly for centuries. It so frequently brought an end to the pain and suffering of the aged and senile that the respected physician Sir William Osler labeled it "the old man's friend." Osler said that pneumonia was nature's way of drawing a veil over a dying person's last hours, to relieve him from suffering and to spare him from watching himself die.

Then, with the development of penicillin and other antibiotics, doctors were able to cure pneumonia. But with this cure, they have saved many patients whose futures hold nothing more than an artificial existence, burdened by both emotional and physical suffering.

Daniel Callahan, director of the Institute of Society, Ethics and the Life Sciences, has frequently discussed this dilemma that society has been placed in by modern medicine. Before a U.S. Senate committee hearing in 1971, Callahan said, "Our homes for the aged are filled with human beings who, but for obsessively effective lifesaving techniques, might long ago have passed to mercifully quick deaths, their faculties still intact.

"Our hospitals are filled with physicians who, precisely because of the new powers given them, are often forced to make decisions far more agonizing than those faced by their predecessors: whether and when to cease treating a dying patient whose life might artificially be extended for an indefinite period; whether to use a miracle drug at the possible price of devastating side effects; whether to try radical brain surgery at the hazard of making a person less than human."

Callahan says that the new problems medicine has raised must be dealt with realistically. "It is increasingly difficult," he told the Senate committee, "for medicine to go forward with a heightened sensitivity to the fact that 'progress' can

8

carry a high price tag, the economic aspects of which may be the least problems."

Many of those most concerned with the issue of euthanasia believe that society is now ready to face the subject squarely. Just as issues like birth control and abortion were openly debated in the 1960s, the controversies surrounding euthanasia are due for redefining in the 1970s. Questions will have to be answered as to whether a terminally ill patient has a legal right to ask that his own life be ended with dignity. Or whether a doctor should maintain a patient who is dead in the human sense, but who is being kept technically "alive" by a machine that keeps his heart and his lungs functioning.

Until these issues are resolved, we will continue to hear stories like the one told by a Los Angeles accountant. His forty-four-year-old wife acquired cancer of the bone of her face. "She was in terrible pain," he says. "The doctors tried radium treatments, but that didn't work. The growths just kept getting bigger and bigger until she could barely talk or swallow. The pain-killing drugs didn't help much, and she really suffered for months until she died.

"So many times she asked me why she couldn't just die, why she had to endure the pain. I didn't have the answer. And when we both really needed to know, no one else could give us the answer either."

2. The Conditions and Justifications for Euthanasia

When doctors and theologians discuss the pros and cons of euthanasia, they generally separate their thinking into two distinct categories: active euthanasia and passive euthanasia.

A doctor who practices passive euthanasia would, for example, supply a dying patient with enough medication to relieve his pain, even if this also contributed to the shortening of his life. Or he would withhold a supportive treatment that might prolong life in a terminal case. This is the most common type of euthanasia, and although technically illegal, it occurs frequently in hospitals. Consider the case of a patient who has suffered brain damage without any hope of recovery, and is being kept alive only with the aid of a cardiac pacemaker and a breathing machine. The doctor, rather than letting the patient exist indefinitely in suspended animation, could choose to act by disconnecting the machinery keeping

11

him alive. Lord Platt, a former president of England's Royal College of Physicians, believes this form of euthanasia is completely justifiable. "In such cases," he once said, "after every possible test has been done, and after full consideration, I think there is general agreement that there comes a time when the apparatus must be switched off."

Active euthanasia is much more controversial, and physicians almost never admit to practicing it. It involves the doctor actively administering a drug or other modality to hasten death. The physician, for example, might intentionally prescribe a lethal overdose of medication to a terminally ill patient. Or he could intravenously inject a substantial quantity of a foreign substance—like air bubbles—into the dying patient to end life.

Carrying these definitions a bit further, both active and passive euthanasia can be administered either voluntarily or involuntarily, depending on whether or not the patient (or his family if he is incapacitated) has consented to the action.

According to hospital spokesmen, the number of patients requesting voluntary euthanasia is increasing. Many of these people are victims of terminal cancer, who are weighed down with severe pain. Although drugs can often ease the pain, they frequently induce a variety of side effects—like nausea, vomiting, and constipation. Many cancer patients are also burdened with difficulty in swallowing, painful and frequent urination, and the mental anguish of watching their bodies deteriorate in what one doctor calls a "death in life."

Take the recent case of a seventy-year-old man suffering from cancer of the bowels. Doctors operated on the cancerous growth, but were unable to completely remove it. The operation did allow the patient three more months of life, but it was an agonizing ending. He became extremely weak, and medication was unable to relieve his vomiting and much

12

of his pain. The patient talked to his doctor about euthanasia several times. Finally, when the pain was so intense, he demanded it, and his wish was granted. Later, his doctor said, "Perhaps he might have lived one more week."

In so many terminal cases, the pain of living sometimes seems worse than death itself. About eight thousand Americans die annually from primary kidney disease. Death can be averted only through transplant, or through treatment on hemodialysis (an artificial kidney machine) which removes poisons from the blood.

Because of a shortage of the proper apparatus, only three thousand Americans a year can receive dialysis care. Yet even those who are in the dialysis program sometimes cannot endure the physical and mental anguish involved in the treatments.

The side effects are often overwhelming. Prolonged dialysis treatment can cause infections, severe headaches, disease of the bones, impotence, arthritis, hepatitis, neurological diseases, and gastrointestinal hemorrhage in patients. The financial burden is also heavy. In 1965, the Veterans Administration Hospital in Denver estimated that the cost per day per dialysis patient was $70.15, because of the many microbiological and chemical processes involved. Today, that figure has almost doubled.

Consequently, some dialysis patients have voluntarily removed themselves from the treatments, despondent over the serious side effects and the financial hardships involved. A post office clerk in his middle fifties knew he would die from uremia poisoning without the blood-purifying action of the kidney machine. But the extended length of the treatments (six hours a day, three times a week) was demoralizing, and the side effects (impotence and severe itching) were more than he could endure. One day, while hooked up to the machine, he decided he had had enough. He pulled the needles out of his arms, and walked out of the hospital. He never went back, and he died a week later.

Another man, age thirty-three, decided to refuse further treatment after three years on the artificial kidney in Detroit. "I'm taking myself off the machine," he told his doctor. "I'm ready to die. I could put up with the blindness and even the pain. But the futility—I mean being inactive and with no chance to do anything—this is the worst of all."

In the 1964 presidential address to the American Society for Artificial Internal Organs, Dr. Belding H. Scribner geared his comments toward the dilemma of the kidney machine. Dr. Scribner, a pioneer in the use of the machine in both the United States and Sweden, explained that the number of patients requesting removal from the dialysis program is likely to increase, although such a decision means certain death. "How much more humane and less expensive it would be," he said, "to offer such a dying patient a weekly hemodialysis for a limited period"—instead of the normal two- or three-times-a-week treatments. "Then he could live a normal life right up to the end and die quickly and without prolonged suffering."

Discouraged hemodialysis patients have used various means of self-destruction when their doctors have refused to agree to discontinuation of their treatments. A few have removed the "shunt" from their bodies, which is the lifeline of the dialysis patient. The shunt is the plastic tubing that is placed in an artery or vein of the patient's lower leg or forearm. When he is attached to the kidney machine, it is actually the shunt which is connected to the apparatus. However, when dialysis patients have become frustrated by the hardships of day-to-day living, some have pulled the shunt from their bodies and have bled to death.

Other patients on dialysis have intentionally wavered from the stringent dietary restrictions placed upon them, like the limitations on liquid consumption, on salt and other spices, and on the types of proteins consumed. This action inevitably throws off the body's chemical and fluid balances, causing death.

According to a study reported in the *American Journal of Psychiatry* (March 1971), 5 percent of all dialysis patients eventually take their own lives by some means.

Some hospitals have made it a matter of policy to respond to the desires of these kidney machine patients—even if it means removing the machinery and letting the patient die, and even if technically they are assisting the patient in committing voluntary passive euthanasia.

At a hospital in the East, the institution's administration has declared that patients "should have complete freedom from coercion in moving either in or out of the [hemodialysis] program." Soon after this policy went into effect, two patients expressed the desire to voluntarily withdraw from the treatments. The hospital's procedure was to put them both through one more dialysis treatment so their bodies would be in good chemical shape, and then ask them if they still wanted to leave the program. The first patient said, "Don't listen to me, that's my uremia talking, not me. I want to stay on the program." But the other still wanted to discontinue, and since the hospital decided that this was an "intellectually free decision," he was allowed to do so.

A growing number of people see euthanasia as a valid alternative in cases where the patient is incapable of deciding his own fate. For example, although a terminally ill person may be in a coma and thus feel no actual pain, he is "alive" only in a technical sense and his family inevitably suffers greatly, watching their loved one slowly die.

15

In a much publicized incident in 1966, President Gursel of Turkey suffered a severe stroke and lapsed into a coma. Doctors admitted that his chances of regaining consciousness were nil. However, Gursel was kept "alive" for more than seven months. Finally, after 218 days in the coma, he died. His political power was transferred without problems, but in a less stable country, such a situation could have created a major crisis.

Also consider the case of a wealthy and elderly Midwestern woman who was admitted to a private New York hospital several years ago. From the day she entered the institution, she did not speak a word or move a muscle. Encephalitis had enveloped her brain and had left her in a comatose state. For five years, the woman lay in an expensive room, tended around the clock by three shifts of nurses. She did not show any progress, and since her brain was dead, there was no chance that she would ever improve. Yet believing that keeping her "alive" was the compassionate thing to do, her family continued the hospitalization.

Finally a physician confronted the relatives and told them how senseless it was to continue treatment any longer. After speaking with a minister, the family agreed that the drugs and nutrients that were keeping her functioning should cease. The woman was finally allowed to die.

"It is wrong for doctors to see how long we can keep 'vegetables' going," the physician said later. "I want no part of it."

For her five years of hospitalization, the woman's medical bills were staggering. But her relatives were fortunate that they had the means to pay the expenses. Other families are not as lucky.

That was the case with an Oklahoma man who died in 1966, eight years after a head-on traffic accident had left him in a permanent semicomatose state, with multiple brain injuries. He never regained full consciousness, but he remained in the hospital year after year, receiving drugs to combat his convulsions and raging fever. Heroic medical action was frequently utilized to battle a recurring urinary infection.

The doctors never considered euthanasia, nor did they discuss it with the patient's wife and daughter. Finally—eight years, eight months, and nineteen days after he had lost consciousness—the man died before corrective action could be taken on improperly circulating blood. The family's ordeal was finally through, although the medical bills still plague them today.

In another case, a patient with irreparable brain damage was kept functioning for nine years with a catheter in his bladder. Deep in a coma, the only way he could be fed was to insert a tube down his throat and transmit the food through it. Three special nurses were hired to care for him around-the-clock in a room that cost $700 a month. After the nine-year ordeal finally ended when the patient died, the total medical expenses came to nearly $300,000.

Advocates of euthanasia are convinced that their ranks will increase as the costs of medical and hospital care continue to spiral. Keeping a person in a state of suspended life is an increasingly expensive venture. In some major cities, patients' bills in hospitals are already up to $110 a day and more, not including extra fees for doctors, specialists, anesthetists, drugs, and even aspirins. Just a few days in a hospital can wipe out a family's life savings.

In Ohio, a fifty-four-year-old machinist was treated for twenty-nine hours and seven minutes in a hospital in a futile attempt to save his life. By the time that relatively short ordeal was over, the medical bills amounted to an unbelievable $7,311.60. The patient, suffering from a serious heart condition, was operated on, and then received the care and attention of eight specially trained doctors, nurses, and technicians. He was given electric shock treatment in hopes of stabilizing his erratic heartbeat. Thirty-one units of blood were transfused into him, in effect replacing his entire blood supply nearly four times. The scandalous hospital bill would even have been more had not some of the specialists on the case waived their fees.

When hospital bills are so outrageously expensive, is it worth the cost and the effort to keep, for example, a patient in an irreversible coma alive?

An elderly woman, now in good health, fears what could happen to her if she should become terminally ill. "How much more joyous the next twenty years would be," she says, "if I could at this time have a private sensible arrangement with my doctor to let me die in peace and dignity instead of squandering my estate keeping alive a nothing."

Some prominent spokesmen think that most doctors are abdicating their responsibility in this area. Henry H. Foster, professor of law at New York University Law School, believes that when people are kept alive by artificial means, this sometimes legally constitutes nothing more than experimentation—making guinea pigs out of humans. "There are a few cases," says Foster, "where doctors have prolonged the life of people in comas for months or years—perhaps out of scientific curiosity, without regard to the financial expense to the family. In a Michigan case, a family lost everything they had—over $160,000 in medical expenses—for keeping alive a member of the family known to have no chance of rehabilitation."

Maintaining a terminally ill patient lingering near death is expensive not only in terms of money. One California hospital administrator claims that his facilities, already overcrowded and understaffed, cannot realistically allocate space and manpower to a hopeless task. "It isn't right that we are channeling so much of our manpower—doctors, nurses, and nurses' aides—toward increasing the quantity of life rather than quality of life," says the hospital executive. "Ideally, these highly trained personnel should be expending their energies on patients who have some hope, who have at least some chance of meaningful life."

Neasden Hospital in northwest London became embroiled in a controversy in 1967 when its staff bulletin board carried this message:

> The following patients are not to be resuscitated: very elderly, over sixty-five, malignant disease. Chronic chest disease. Chronic renal disease.
> Top of yellow treatment card to be marked NTBR (i.e., Not To Be Resuscitated).
> The following people should be resuscitated: collapse as a result of diagnostic or therapeutic procedures—e.g., needle in pleura (even if over sixty-five years). Sudden unexpected collapse under sixty-five—i.e., loss of consciousness, cessation of breathing, no cartoid pulsation.

The message was signed by Neasden's medical superintendent, Dr. W. F. T. McMath, and was directed to all physicians and nurses at the hospital. The public uproar over the statement led the British Minister of Health to appoint a board of inquiry to investigate the matter. Although many doctors in England openly defended Dr. McMath, the official inquiry condemned him for rejecting resuscitation in certain patients simply because of their age.

Dr. Kenneth O. A. Vickery, an English physician, made world headlines two years later when he dealt with the same subject in a speech before the Royal Society of Health. Dr. Vickery said that due to overloaded hospital conditions,

19

doctors should be relieved of their moral responsibility to keep aged patients alive as long as possible. He argued that "in a community which can no longer adequately nurse all its chronic sick and where beds are so blocked by the aged that younger people requiring surgical and medical treatment cannot be admitted, we can no longer avoid the issue of medicated survival."

The speech by Dr. Vickery came just five weeks after the death of former President Eisenhower at Walter Reed Army Hospital, and the British doctor cited that case as "the most dreadful example of medicated survival." Eisenhower had suffered six heart attacks and underwent two major operations in the last four years of his life. Just prior to his death, he clung to life only through the use of oxygen, drugs to vitalize his heart, and other drugs to clear his body of excess salt and water.

Only sedatives and "good nursing" should have been given to Eisenhower, said Dr. Vickery. He criticized all the other life-sustaining techniques used on the former president, adding, "If this is to be the case for the rest of society, we are in for a hell of a time."

Dr. Vickery suggested that "the time has come for a minimum age to be agreed beyond which medical and nursing staffs may be relieved of the prevailing obligation 'officiously to keep alive' and confine their ministrations to symptomatic relief and good nursing." He recommended eighty as the minimum age beyond which doctors should stop "resuscitating the dying."

The speech was met with mixed but loud reactions. Even strong advocates of euthanasia said they could not accept Dr. Vickery's arbitrary cut-off age of eighty, claiming instead that each individual case should be considered on its own merits, no matter what the age of the patient.

Probably the most poignant support for Dr. Vickery came from elderly people themselves. The doctor received literally thousands of letters from the aged who longed to die peacefully. A man wrote from an institution in West Germany, where he lay crippled with arthritis, as well as having lost his senses of hearing and taste. He was also suffering from dropsy caused by heart and kidney failures. He told of how doctors had plucked him from death many times, and how he dreaded the large needles used for his daily injections of iron. He said that he constantly prayed to die.

A New York woman wrote of how her brave grandmother had endured unmerciful suffering during nineteen years in a nursing home. The old woman had literally wasted away while doctors brought her back from death time and time again. She ultimately died in the fetal position at age ninety-six, and was buried in a child's-size coffin.

A nurse wrote from Middlesex, in the midst of her tenth year of caring for her eighty-seven-year-old mother, who was suffering from chronic heart and kidney disease. The mother had survived three strokes. She had also suffered a respiratory collapse which resulted from a skin graft operation needed to correct acute bed sores. Doctors applied heart massage and a blood transfusion to pull the woman through. As she wrote the letter, the daughter was being asked to approve a colostomy operation for her mother to overcome an intestinal obstruction.

Another letter came from a woman in Norfolk, England, who said that she had suffered both mental and physical exhaustion during the last years of her mother's life. The mother had been healthy until age eighty-four, when she suffered a stroke and subsequently pneumonia. When she "recovered," she was severely paralyzed, permanently confined to a bed, and completely dependent upon her daughter.

The woman explained that her mother's mental alertness began to deteriorate, and soon she became aggressive and unmanageable. For the next five years until the old woman died, the daughter said the ordeal that she herself went through drained her of all the love and tenderness she had once felt for her mother.

This type of heavy psychological toll upon the relatives of a dying patient is not unusual. The ordeal of a prolonged dying process is often as painful for the family looking on as it is for the patient himself.

A nurse in a California hospital recalls the way one husband reacted to the prolonged dying of his wife. "When the patient was first admitted to the hospital," she recalls, "her husband seemed to have pretty good control of himself. But as he saw her deteriorate over the days, his mental condition drastically worsened. Watching her suffer so much was quite a strain on him.

"We resuscitated her twice, and looking back, I don't really know why. We knew her case was hopeless. Sometimes I think it might be better to let patients like her just die as comfortably as possible. It would probably be easier that way for both the patients and their families."

A New York woman admits that she has yet to fully recover from the emotional crisis of watching her husband die of cancer. She says her readjustment has been difficult, even though two years have passed since the death of her spouse. "I saw such great suffering for so long, I have been unable to make a proper readjustment, even though I consider myself to be a well-balanced person. I am still haunted and troubled by the suffering I was unable to prevent.

"Twofold suffering can result from antiquated beliefs about prolonging life in those we love," she says. "I am trying hard to overcome the disastrous effects upon my own

22

life, having lived with such suffering, but have moments of thinking that two good lives went at the same time."

A Florida man and wife recently went through the terrible trauma of a prolonged fatal illness. The couple, whom we shall call Robert and Eileen, endured together her drawn-out death from cancer. They had received the diagnosis of terminal cancer in January, and when Eileen entered the hospital for the fourth time in September, her doctors told Robert that she would die within two hours if she were not operated on immediately. "I couldn't refuse," recalls Robert. "It would haunt me, I think . . . refusing. I know I would have wondered later if the operation would have saved her. My back was to the wall. I told them to go ahead. What would you have done? They rushed up to her room, knocked her out, and put the knives into her."

The operation left Eileen with a four-inch wound in her stomach, and when she was released to go home in another month, she weighed just seventy pounds. The pain pills that she was given caused her to hallucinate. She once told Robert she saw red bugs crawling throughout their bedroom. Another time, she saw long strands of hair floating in the air above her.

Just before Eileen finally died, Robert reflected for a moment and said, "Since January, we have had a mass said for her each month. Up until the last few months, they were said for her recovery. Now they are being said for her death.

"It sounds awful, I know. But she suffers so. You have no idea. Six or seven months ago, we could walk together. Now it's different. You watch this happen to a person you love and eventually you grow cold. I know that if she had died four months ago, it would have torn me apart. Now her death will bring sorrow, but it will come as a relief."

And would Robert have allowed his wife to have had

another operation if it would have given her a few more weeks of life? "I wouldn't have allowed it," he said. "It would have served no purpose."

The overwhelming majority of elderly people apparently agree with Robert. In a 1970 study conducted by the University of Southern California Gerontology Center, 90 percent of the older persons surveyed said they would not want "heroic" medical techniques used on them if they were on the brink of death.

The participants in the study, conducted by former Presbyterian minister James T. Mathieu, were 183 residents of a Southern California retirement home, ranging in age from fifty to eighty-six. More than 60 percent of them favored "withdrawal of all treatments except those designed to maintain comfort and reduce pain." Another 30 percent said they would accept "reasonable life-maintaining treatment," as long as it fell short of heroic treatment. Only 4 percent of those questioned said they would want their doctors to use every known medical treatment to keep them alive.

A physical therapist in an Arizona hospital says that she has found that most terminally ill patients would like to be left alone to die peacefully. "We are keeping people alive long beyond the point when they should have been allowed to die with dignity," she explains.

"Frequently they ask me why they go through so much pain and discomfort just to prolong something so inevitable. Doctors often don't even consult the patient himself. They just prescribe certain treatment that nurses and therapists are supposed to carry out. Sometimes weeks will go by and the patient won't ever have a chance to speak to his doctor.

"I've held the hands of patients who are dying, and who are so weak that they can't even speak," she continues. "Yet after a while you can tell just by looking in their eyes that they're ready to die, and that they've been ready to go for a long time.

"If we let people choose the condition of their own dying, I think many of the hopelessly ill would choose to die peacefully without any senseless life-prolonging techniques being applied. The patient should carry the weightiest voice in such matters, yet he's often never even consulted."

Such sentiment is leading thousands of Americans to sign a statement—called a "living will"—which is distributed by a New York-based organization called the Euthanasia Educational Fund. The will requests that its signer be allowed to "die with dignity" if he should become terminally ill. It states:

> To my family physician, my clergyman, my lawyer—
> If the time comes when I can no longer take part in decisions for my own future, let this statement stand as a testament of my wishes:
> If there is no reasonable expectation of my recovery from physical or mental disability, I request that I be allowed to die and not be kept alive by artificial means or heroic measures. Death is as much a reality as birth, growth, maturity, and old age—it is the one certainty. I do not fear death as much as I fear the indignity of deterioration, dependence and hopeless pain. I ask that drugs be mercifully administered to me for terminal suffering even if they hasten the moment of death.
> This request is made after careful consideration. Although this document is not legally binding, you who care for me will, I hope, feel morally bound to follow its mandate. I recognize that it places a heavy burden of responsibility upon you, and it is with the intention of sharing that responsibility and of mitigating any feelings of guilt that this statement is made.

As the living will itself states, it is not a legally binding document. But proponents of the will believe it is valuable in that it helps to relieve the burden of guilt from doctors and families.

Elizabeth T. Halsey, executive director of the Euthanasia Educational Fund, says, "It is mainly a persuasive document. Without it, the family is usually hesitant, which, in turn, holds back the doctor. He's afraid that the family may later sue him for malpractice. Or he often thinks he is trained to keep someone going as long as he possibly can. The 'living will' exists simply to say, 'I don't want to be kept going as long as modern medicine will keep me going. I only want to be kept going as long as I have some reasonable chance of recovery.' "

The Euthanasia Educational Fund is a nonprofit educational organization that gives financial aid to studies and seminars on euthanasia. It advocates euthanasia, but only when that word is defined as the right to die with dignity. "What we're talking about is a voluntary passive euthanasia," says Mrs. Halsey. "We want to allow people who are in a terminal illness not to have their dying process prolonged, not to have heroic measures used on them to keep them alive artificially when there is no future, when there is no 'person' there anymore."

Mrs. Halsey believes that none of the laws against euthanasia will change until public opinion makes an open shift in its favor. "Up until very recently," she says, "no one would even talk about death, let alone euthanasia. What we have been trying to do is to get more people to realize and admit that they're going to die sometime, and it might be sensible to think about it a little ahead of time, and not just let it come on them."

3. The Legal Aspects of Euthanasia

Mrs. Carmen Martinez, a seventy-two-year-old Cuban refugee, lay near death in a Florida hospital in the summer of 1971. She was suffering from hemolytic anemia, and in a desperate attempt to keep her alive, doctors were performing continuous blood transfusions via the "cutdown" method, in which the skin is surgically opened and blood is driven into the veins. After two months of these treatments, which caused unyielding pain, she asked to be allowed to die. "Please don't let them torture me anymore," she told her daughters.

But her doctor refused to yield to Mrs. Martinez's request. He was uneasy about the consequences no matter what action he took. He felt that he might be charged with assisting a suicide if he let his patient die, yet he also believed he was violating her civil rights by refusing to let her decide her own fate.

The doctor brought the case to court, and a judge ruled in favor of Mrs. Martinez. "This woman has a right not to be hurt," said Judge David Popper of the Dade County Circuit Court. "She has a right to live and die in dignity."

Shortly after the decision was handed down, the transfusions were stopped. A day later, Mrs. Martinez died.

Ultimately, the controversy surrounding euthanasia will be decided in the legislatures and in the courts. The landmark Florida case resolved some important questions about a person's right to control his own destiny. The court ruled that voluntary euthanasia was justified under certain circumstances, regardless of the statutory laws against it.

But despite this precedent-setting case, the legal statutes outlawing euthanasia remain unchanged. According to present law, every life is to be preserved as long as possible— no matter what its quantity or quality. Therefore, a doctor who injects a lethal dosage of drugs—even with his patient's consent—could be charged with murder. Even a doctor who withholds treatment and thus speeds up the death of a patient may incur civil liability for his failure to act.

In discussing the issue of active euthanasia, New York attorney Morris Ploscowe wrote in the *New York University Law Review* (November 1956), "Euthanasia is unquestionably unjustifiable homicide under existing statutes. Premeditation, the basic element in murder, is present. Moreover, the fact that the person to be killed is already dying is no justification."

The legal status of euthanasia is quite complicated, though, because there is no universally accepted criteria of death. The Medical Society of New York State, for example, has already declared that "every human being of adult years and sound mind" has a right to determine what shall be done with his own "body" after death. But there is no clear definition of when a person becomes a "body." Is he a "body" once extraordinary methods—like an artificial machine—are needed to keep his heart beating, and thus should he be allowed to decide whether or not to turn the machine off? Is "life" something more than just a beating heart?

Most states have no legal definition of the moment of death—either statutory or within case law. One frequently applied definition, though, is the cessation of heartbeat and respiration. It is stated as follows in *Black's Law Dictionary:*

> The cessation of life; the ceasing to exist; defined by physicians as a total stoppage of the circulation of the blood and a cessation of the animal and vital functions consequent thereon, such as respiration, pulsation, etc.

As recently as twenty-five years ago, determining death was a relatively simple matter. Once a person's breathing and heartbeat had ceased, he was pronounced dead. In some cases, drugs like epinephrine could be injected, but they rarely prolonged life more than just a few minutes. Until recent years, some medical textbooks actually still recommended that death be determined by using a mirror or a feather to ascertain whether exhalation was still continuing.

But today, doctors can revive both respiration and heartbeat after they have stopped, and keep them functioning literally forever. However, if there has been inadequate oxygenation of the blood during the period of heart stoppage, irreparable brain damage invariably results. Even though the heart can be restored to proper functioning, there is no way to correct the brain impairment, thus leaving the patient in a permanent "vegetable" state. Because more people than ever before are now doomed to such a condition, euthanasia is gaining support as a valid release in these cases.

The era of transplants has further complicated the definition of death. For in the case of heart transplantation, if any reasonable chance of success is to exist, the heart must still be beating at the time it is removed from the donor's body. In previous transplants, the donor's heart and circulation have been maintained artificially through the use of a heart-lung machine until surgeons are ready for surgery to begin. However, under Black's legal definition of death, can the donor be considered "dead" if his heartbeat and circulation are still functioning? The answer is obviously no. Early in the transplant age, the deputy district attorney of Los Angeles expressed a belief that transplant surgeons are committing murder because of the questionable legality of the death standards they used.

Thus, some medical authorities believe that a new legal definition of death should be devised, centered around the brain. Since the brain controls the identity and the personality of the human being, it has been suggested that we determine the end of life by the cessation of the brain's electrical activity, as measured by an electroencephalogram (EEG). This could put an end to the countless number of hopeless cases of people lying in a comatose state for weeks, months, and even years, with functioning heart and lungs but a dead brain.

Dr. Robert S. Schwab, professor of neurology at the Harvard Medical School, agrees that the brain should be used as another criterion of death, in addition to the heartbeat. In a 1969 speech to the Second Euthanasia Conference in New York, Dr. Schwab said, "In 99 percent of cases, death can be determined when breathing stops and the heart stops. But there are more and more electronic gadgets all the time to keep the heart going. So you have to have another criterion . . . When the brain stops functioning and has no potential recovery, we define this as irreversible coma. The person, in our concept, is dead—even though he may have an active functioning pump in his chest maintained by apparatus."

Dr. Schwab, who is also head of the Brain Wave Laboratory at Massachusetts General Hospital, has collected three thousand records of cases where the electroencephalograph was utilized to determine death. "Without exception, they are all the same," he says. "The person could make no recovery. We've also had several hundred examinations of such brains at postmortem, and there is no question that there is nothing in the way of living tissue. . . . We're backed in this knowledge of the anatomy of the brain. Brain cells do not regenerate. You can regenerate liver cells, you can grow skin, but unlike the lizard, the human being cannot grow new limbs. So it is with the brain."

In 1968, a faculty committee of the Harvard Medical School recommended that death should be defined as a "permanently nonfunctioning brain." The committee decided that even if the heart and other organs continue to function by artificial means, once the brain has stopped, the patient can be considered dead.

That same year, Dr. Denton Cooley of Houston, Texas, who at that time had performed more heart transplants than any other man, met with twelve other transplant surgeons at the Cape Town Conference on Heart Transplants. After the conference had ended, Dr. Cooley told the press, "On the sticky question of how to determine the donor's death, there was no heated controversy, probably because all of us had answered this question for ourselves a long time ago. We agreed that neurological examination and electroencephalograph tracings should show no signs of cerebral activity, but did not define the length of time this should be so. In most heart transplants performed to date, this period exceeded two hours. In two of my donors, there was a flattened EEG for four days prior to transplantation. . . ."

Life magazine (August 2, 1968) quoted Dr. Cooley as saying, "The heart has always been a special organ. It has been considered the seat of the soul, the source of courage. But I look upon the heart only as a pump, a servant of the brain. Once the brain is gone, the heart becomes unemployed. Then we must find it other employment."

However, there are unresolved questions even in using the EEG to define death. As Dr. Cooley says, there is no agreement on how long an EEG reading must be a straight line before a person is to be considered dead. What is meant by a *permanently* nonfunctioning brain? As yet, this dilemma is still unresolved.

Several medical committees have stated that death can be pronounced twenty-four hours after the flat EEG has begun. A panel of the American Encephalographic Society has suggested that only a two-hour wait is needed. A study at Johns Hopkins concluded that the first indication of a flat EEG signifies death.

In 1970, Kansas became the first state to enact a statute which provides simply that the "absence of spontaneous brain function" is a criterion of death.

The Kansas law says that:

A person shall be regarded as medically dead if in the opinion of a physician based on ordinary standards of medical practice, there is absence of spontaneous brain function; and if based on ordinary standards of medical practice during reasonable attempts to either maintain or restore spontaneous circulatory or respiratory function in the absence of a foresaid brain function, it appears that further attempts at resuscitation or supportive maintenance will not succeed, death will have occurred at the time when these conditions first coincide.

Thus, according to the Kansas law, a person is considered dead when his brain waves cease, even if his heart and breathing are kept functioning by mechanical devices.

In 1972, a Virginia court jury decided that once the brain has ceased to operate, then a person is dead. The case involved doctors at the Medical College of Virginia, who were accused of turning off the respirator of fifty-six-year-old Bruce Tucker, whose heart continued to beat artificially after his brain waves had stopped. The family sued the doctors for "wrongfully killing" Tucker and transplanting his heart into another patient.

Tucker, who had suffered a severe brain hemorrhage in a fall, had shown only weak signs of life when he was rushed to the hospital. Five hours after he arrived at the emergency facility, surgery was performed to relieve brain hemorrhaging and swelling. A tracheotomy had to be performed to ease his breathing. After surgery, intravenous feeding was ordered, and eventually the patient had to be placed on a respirator.

Doctors had noted in the hospital record that the "prognosis for recovery is nil and death is imminent." A neurologist ran an electroencephalograph test for twenty-five minutes, and after that and other tests, he concluded that the patient's brain was dead.

While the respirator kept Tucker functioning, attempts were made to locate his family. But his relatives could not be reached, and thirteen hours after the brain surgery, the attending physician disconnected the respirator and pronounced the patient dead.

Before the Tucker case went to the jury, Judge A.

Christian Compton told the court of his own beliefs, that death to him occurs only when there is a total stoppage of breathing, pulse, and circulation, indicating he felt the doctors were guilty of wrongdoing. He said that it was not a job for the courts to determine the legal definition of death, that it should be a matter for legislatures to decide. He predicted chaos in the legal world if the jury supported the concept of brain death.

However, Judge Compton still encouraged the jury to make up its own mind—and it did. It took the jury only seventy-one minutes to acquit the doctors and decide that irreversible loss of brain function was a valid indication of death. Because of the decision, some doctors say they now feel somewhat freer to turn off the respirator—thus committing passive euthanasia—once cerebral death has been clearly determined.

Although this court case will likely influence the course of euthanasia over the upcoming years, does it go far enough? Shouldn't other factors—nonmedical ones—be considered when doctors determine whether a life should be prolonged? Joseph Fletcher, professor of medical and social ethics at Episcopal Theological School, believes so.

"Just redefining death in terms of encephalogram readings and deoxygenation of the brain or losses of spontaneous organ function elsewhere in the system and so on—this is not enough," says Fletcher.

"Is the question of when we have lost the human being— not the biological system, but the human being—something that has to be answered in terms of such criteria or components as cerebration, memory, a sense of futurity, some evident chemical capacity for interpersonal relationship, will or purpose? Lovingness—is this in the catalog? A minimum

IQ? Utilitarian questions about social productivity and its potential?

"We all talk rather slickly, especially in the theological and philosophical tradition about the *humanum*, but when you try to get down to brass tacks to say, to specify, to itemize the component elements of the *humanum*, they fade away. We, in our society, owe it to our physicians to help them elaborate some kind of rational and operable understanding of this question. At the terminal end of the human cycle, is there a human being present or recoverable, and not just life in the biological sense?"

Definitions of death and euthanasia are as legally complex in some other countries as they are in the United States. Since the Suicide Act of 1961 became law in England, it is no longer a crime for a person, either healthy or ill, to kill himself or attempt to do so. However, anyone who assists him in the act—like a doctor administering voluntary euthanasia—could be charged with manslaughter, punishable by imprisonment of up to fourteen years. Even a doctor who acts in good faith to mercifully release a patient from a hopelessly ill state is still guilty of an offense.

England's Royal Commission on Capital Punishment has stated "reluctantly" that it cannot recommend legalization of even voluntary euthanasia. The commission has proclaimed that it would be "impossible to define a category [of mercy killing] which could not be seriously abused."

However, a precedent has been set in England in which a doctor is not to be held criminally liable if he gives a patient the minimum dosage of a drug necessary to relieve pain, even if that dosage is fatal. In 1957, a British court found a doctor innocent of murder when he prescribed a pain-relieving drug which killed his patient. In that case, the jury was instructed by the presiding judge as follows: "If the first purpose of medicine, the restoration of health, can no longer be achieved there is still much for a doctor to do, and he is entitled to do all that is proper and necessary to relieve pain and suffering, even if the measures he takes may incidentally shorten human life."

In both France and Belgium, euthanasia is considered premeditated homicide. German law is somewhat more lenient, not regarding as normal homicide the "physician's failure to prolong artificially an expiring painful life by applying stimulants." The German penal code has a special provision for "homicide upon the request of the person killed." When the victim has requested the action, the maximum punishment for the mercy-killer is two years, with a reduction down to six months if extenuating circumstances are present.

Scottish law considers euthanasia to be murder, although in practice it is rarely regarded as more serious than "culpable homicide." In fact, no physician in Scotland has ever been prosecuted for murder by euthanasia. However, technically, even if the patient has consented to the euthanasia, the doctor is not relieved of all legal responsibility. According to the High Court of Justiciary in Scotland, ". . . if life is taken under circumstances which would otherwise infer guilt of murder, the crime does not cease to be murder merely because the victim consented to be murdered, or even urged the assailant to strike the fatal blow."

Sweden permits passive euthanasia in the form of withdrawal of life-support therapy from patients considered to be dying hopelessly. Russia considers euthanasia "murder under extenuating circumstances" and punishable by three to eight years in prison. Uruguay allows a "compassionate homicide," administered at the request of the patient, which leaves the doctors free of all prosecution.

The Swiss penal code was revised in 1951, legalizing passive euthanasia and thus allowing doctors to withhold life-sustaining medication in hopeless cases. Also, a physician who makes a poison available to a dying patient is not breaking the law, providing he does not administer it himself.

Even a Swiss doctor who actively injects a lethal agent into a terminally ill patient is charged with manslaughter rather than murder. This lesser charge is applicable when the offender has not exhibited inhumane behavior in his action. The Swiss believe that the true murderer has a depraved mind, and is a danger to society. A doctor who administers euthanasia out of compassion does not exhibit these characteristics.

In Norway, too, the motives of the doctor are given consideration by the court. Sentences can be reduced considerably if the victim was hopelessly ill. The Norwegian penal code also provides special treatment when the action was committed with the victim's consent. In cases where the victim has consented to his own euthanasia, and where the doctor was motivated by mercy in taking the life, the punishment may be reduced well below that outlined in existing statutes.

There are indications now that there may be changes in the euthanasia laws on both sides of the Atlantic. Sentiment among many influential voices is leaning toward a liberalization of existing statutes. A convocation of the American Assembly at Arden House, with people like Dr. Russell Nelson of the American Association of Medical Colleges, and Judge Russell Marvin Frankel of the New York Federal District Court in attendance, has adopted the following statement: "We should make a study of whether suicide and other laws can be modified to enable victims of terminal illness to avoid the unwelcome prolongation of life with assistance and without penalty."

A conference of the American Humanist Association has passed one of the most far-reaching resolutions dealing with the subject:

> The Right to Personality: Men and women today are living longer than formerly, but this does not mean, necessarily, less suffering at the end of life, when deterioration is often prolonged, to the point that personality is lost in senility and incurable suffering.
>
> Therefore, be it resolved that the American Humanist Association endorses legalized euthanasia in principle and urges that individual Humanists support laws which assure that:
>
> 1. Any person beset by incurable suffering may legally petition for release;
>
> 2. All proper and possible safeguards against misuse of the law be provided and that doctors involved shall be free from public condemnation;
>
> 3. Any human being should be protected in his free choice to die before senility sets in;
>
> 4. Medieval inherited laws now widely prevalent which make suicide a crime should be rescinded.

Political leaders, too, are making public statements. Early in 1972, Oregon's Governor Tom McCall met with his state's delegation to the White House Conference on Aging. "Oregon's delegates told me that thousands of persons of advanced years are haunted by the prospect of drawn-out deaths," says McCall. "Concern was expressed over lingering hospitalization for months and even years in a hopeless semicoma, and leaving the surviving spouse exhausted, desperate, and bankrupt."

Shortly after his meeting with the delegation, McCall spoke before a conference of four hundred Republicans, at which he called for a study into the subject of euthanasia. "I don't know whether you will get into the subject of death with dignity at this conference," he said, "but you'll need to soon because it is an unclear right that somehow must be made more visible and legally available."

According to McCall, "There ought to be a legal way to provide death with dignity in one's advanced years, as opposed to life as a vegetable. There's no chance of having any savings left for a surviving spouse who may have to go on welfare, lonely, sad, bankrupt."

After the speech, McCall's office was flooded with letters from people referring to the governor as everything from "a man of compassion" to "the new Hitler of Oregon." And McCall admits that he was not totally surprised by the widespread public reaction to his address. "I immediately sensed the volatility of the issue, saying that anyone who raised it would be misunderstood and criticized, but that I would move, even so, to open a public dialog on it. My hope was, and is, that I can sponsor a symposium to work toward reducing the problem to rational, instead of emotional, terms."

Much of the mail that McCall received was favorable to his cause. A student nurse wrote, "I am ready to climb the walls, watching my terminal patients being kept alive with tubes down their noses, intravenous feedings, and intravenous blood feedings to bring them back to reality, and suffering until they cannot stand it any longer."

One woman encouraged the governor to keep speaking out on the subject of euthanasia. "You will be vilified," she wrote, "but you also will be blessed." A letter writer from California said, "If you succeed in writing mercy killing into Oregon's laws, I plan to come to Oregon to live."

Dr. O. Ruth Russell, professor emeritus of psychology at Western Maryland University, has recommended that legislation be enacted that would permit a patient's next of kin to request that the patient's life be ended if he is mentally incapable of making such a decision himself.

The Bill of Rights Committee of the Montana State Constitutional Convention has debated the inclusion of a "right to die" provision in the state's new constitution. The committee heard testimony from dozens of people, but was particularly moved by a plea from Mrs. Joyce Franks, who described how her father died "for eight weeks, little by little, minute by minute." She told how he had begged to be put to death quickly and peacefully, but that his doctor refused. "I maintain," she said, "that to give to people facing certain death the right to die quickly, easily, and in peace when they want to do so, is being compassionate, intelligent, and human."

Although the Bill of Rights Committee eventually declined to include the "right to die" provision in the new constitution, Mrs. Franks continues to spearhead the drive in Montana for changes in the euthanasia laws.

"Since the day Dad first asked me for euthanasia," says Mrs. Franks, "I have been fighting toward legalizing the self-determined usage of it. He was in his eighty-sixth year, having been more dead than alive for four years really. He could hardly see across the room. He couldn't read or walk. He couldn't hear well enough to understand what was going on around him. And worst of all, he couldn't talk. He couldn't even cry or holler to get someone else's attention.

"Then he broke his hip," she recalls. "With his arms and legs skinless from the experience of total bedridden dependence, and more than ever unable to communicate with us—let alone the doctor or the world—he asked for the doctor to give him pills to let him go. Of course he was denied them. So he was condemned by society to suffer the degradation and debasement of total dependency, much worse than that of babyhood, for eight more weeks before God finally saw fit to stop his stubborn heart which had so long insisted on pumping on the dry well of his life."

Residents of Pilgrim Place, a retirement home in Claremont, California, have been some of the strongest advocates of changes in current euthanasia legislation. In the spring of 1972, they presented a petition with 166 signatures to attorneys and legislators, urging that a state law be enacted to free from prosecution those doctors who refuse to needlessly prolong the life of hopelessly ill patients.

The Reverend Richard Steiner, a former Unitarian pastor who now lives in the sixty-five-and-older retirement community, says that the "death with dignity" movement began there after one of its residents died following a lingering and painful illness.

"The manner of his dying with artificial aids to prolong his life for a few days—when there was no hope of recovery from the cancer which he suffered—so agitated his devoted wife that after his death she determined to find some avenue by which others might be spared the burden," recalls Reverend Steiner.

A committee was formed at Pilgrim Place, which drew up the petition urging California lawmakers to enact legislation to protect physicians "from civil suits or criminal prosecution if they fail to use surgical, medical, or mechanical procedures for the prolongation of life on those who are terminally ill, permitting them to die with dignity according to the will of God, with confidence in eternal life."

One of the signers of the petition recalls her own husband's painful dying from terminal cancer: "Every time I came back to the hospital, he said, 'This is the end, I've had it, I just can't go on. Help me to go quickly.' I requested the doctor to do so, but he couldn't do anything. Those days were very hard to bear."

The same elderly woman says that most of her friends fear

41

such a needlessly prolonged dying process. "What we dread more than anything else," she explains, "is to become just a vegetable, a nonperson, and then have to be cared for month after month until the heart stops beating. Of course, real life has gone long before that. When the mind has died, life has ended. Real life does not exist after the brain is not active. So why waste the resources—they're becoming more and more scarce on this earth—just keeping the heart beating in a 'life' that is gone?"

Says another resident of Pilgrim Place, "I don't mind dying, but I do mind the way I'm going to die, and I don't want to die without dignity. There are worse things than dying and one of them can be living—living in pain."

There have already been several instances where euthanasia bills have been introduced in state legislatures, but they have all been defeated. In 1937, a bill to legalize euthanasia was put before Nebraska's lawmakers, but it never got out of committee. A similar bill was introduced in the New York State General Assembly in 1947, but it also died in committee. The New York bill proposed the following:

—Any sane person over twenty-one, suffering from a painful and deadly disease, may request that euthanasia be administered to him. The request would come on a signed and attested document, accompanied by an affidavit from the attending physician that he has diagnosed the disease as incurable;

—A commission of three—at least two of whom must be physicians—would be appointed by the court to investigate all aspects of the case. The commission would report back to the court as to whether the patient fully understands the implications of the petition, and whether the request falls under the provisions of the act;

—If the commission report is favorable, the court shall approve the petition, and if euthanasia is still desired by the patient, it may be administered by a physician or any other person selected by the patient or the commission.

Although the New York bill would have undoubtedly been defeated if it had ever reached a vote in the full legislature, many advocates of euthanasia felt that the bill was not strong enough. They claimed that it was limited in scope, since it offered no relief to persons under the age of twenty-one, or to those of unsound mind. The so-called vegetable case was not covered by the bill.

In the legislature of the state of Washington, a euthanasia bill was introduced in 1968 by Arval Morris, a professor of law, but it failed to pass. It would have provided for a declaration that could be signed by a patient, requesting that death be allowed or induced if he should become irreparably impaired either physically or mentally. Thirty days after the request, two physicians could approve the patient's wish, and euthanasia would be administered. At any time, the patient could cancel his request, either orally or in writing.

Dr. Walter W. Sackett, a Miami physician and a member of the Florida House of Representatives, has been a consistent advocate of a "death with dignity" provision in his state. In session after session, he has introduced such a bill, but thus far with negative results.

Dr. Sackett, who is a Catholic, believes that the dramatic progress of medicine in recent years has taught the medical profession more about keeping people alive than about keeping them well. He contends that the only life worth preserving is meaningful life.

In 1968, Dr. Sackett proposed an amendment to the Basic

Rights Article of the Florida Constitution at a special Constitutional Revision Session of the legislature. If it had passed, the revised article would have read, in part:

> All natural persons are equal before the law and have inalienable rights, among which are the right to enjoy and defend life, liberty, *to be permitted to die with dignity,* to pursue happiness . . .

After this unsuccessful effort, Dr. Sackett drafted a bill that he has tried unsuccessfully to push through the legislature since 1969. Dr. Sackett advocates that a person be able to legally sign a document stating that he wishes to die with dignity and does not want his life prolonged "beyond the point of a terminal existence." If the attending physician then determines that the patient's condition is in fact hopeless and terminal, all medication and artificial means of sustaining life would cease. If the individual were not mentally capable of deciding, a majority of his closest family members could make the decision in his place. In cases where the patient has no next of kin, a committee of three doctors could make the decision after verifying that there was no chance for long-term survival.

Although Dr. Sackett's bill is not yet law, it has received enthusiastic support from elderly people fearful of a prolonged and painful fatal illness. Backing has also come from people who have watched a relative die in a needlessly undignified way.

One woman wrote to Dr. Sackett, "A few years ago my family and I were subjected to unforgettable suffering caused by the doctor treating my aunt. She was hospitalized with terminal cancer. Her veins had collapsed, making it impossible to insert a needle effectively for intravenous feeding or blood transfusions. The anguish of seeing her abused by this futile probing was unbearable. My family was close to a breakdown by the time she passed away.

"At one point I consulted with the doctor. He had already informed us it was only a matter of time. I pleaded with him to stop the senseless torture, but he remained adamant. Wouldn't it have been more humane to ease her toward a more comfortable end?"

Dr. Sackett also heard from a Florida state employee whose husband spent the last sixteen years of his life in a coma, kept "alive" by sophisticated medical machines. The woman described how she worked for those sixteen years, only to have her earnings pulverized by medical bills to keep a hopeless "vegetable" functioning. Dr. Sackett believes that the tragedy of this particular case involved two lives—not just one. The patient's life had no meaning, and under the circumstances, neither did his wife's.

"It really doesn't take much to convince a next of kin how important a dignified death is," says Dr. Sackett. "I just pose the question to the relative, 'Now, that's you lying there, what do you want?' The response is invariably, 'Oh, doctor, let me go.' "

Although his actions are technically illegal, Dr. Sackett admits that in his thirty years of practice, he has "let hundreds of patients go."

"There is no putting to death in what I'm proposing," he says, referring to his bill. "There is no life in a meaningful sense in many terminally ill people. A person in a coma is not enjoying life, and in fact, he may be shattering the lives of members of his family."

But most lawmakers have hesitated to show any open support for Dr. Sackett's legislation or any other euthanasia proposals. "Legislators on the whole have been very shy to advocate any legislation," says Elizabeth Halsey of the Euthanasia Educational Fund. "They're running for election, and they don't see why they should stick their necks out on a very controversial subject until they're convinced that enough of their constituents support the measure."

Yet Dr. Sackett says that several legislators have privately told him of their support for his bill. Some have even suggested that he would receive greater support for the measure if he introduced it only during off-election years.

This same kind of hesitancy on the part of lawmakers is occurring in England, too. The Voluntary Euthanasia Society, a London counterpart of the American euthanasia group, has been trying unsuccessfully to push a euthanasia bill through Parliament since the first one was introduced in 1936. However, support for the legislation among members of Parliament is considerably stronger today than it was for the earlier bills, although the 1936 proposal received enthusiastic promotion from such prominent public figures as Dr. Julian Huxley, Lord Moynihan (president of the Royal College of Surgeons), H. G. Wells, and George Bernard Shaw.

The 1936 bill, which was debated in the House of Lords, would have permitted voluntary euthanasia under certain circumstances. The major objections to the measure came from lawmakers who felt that the various safeguards provided for in the bill would stifle a hospital's normal proceedings with too many legal formalities.

The bill was turned down by a thirty-five to fourteen vote. Even Lord Dawson of Penn, who had been one of Parliament's long-time proponents of a more humane treatment for dying patients, eventually opposed the bill. Though he had frequently stated publicly that the act of dying should be made more gentle and peaceful, he decided that the controversy surrounding the bill was too widespread to warrant his support for the measure.

Yet in the debate over the bill, Dawson told his parliamentary colleagues that doctors have other duties besides just prolonging lives. It is now generally accepted, he said, that physicians must also alleviate pain. He talked about "the gap"—that period of waiting for death by a person suffering from a terminal disease. "There is in the aggregate an unexpressed growth of feeling that the shortening of the gap should not be denied when the real need is there," he explained. "This is due not to a diminution of courage, but rather to a truer conception of what life means and what the end of its usefulness deserves."

In 1950, another motion in favor of voluntary euthanasia was debated by the House of Lords, but it was tabled before a vote was ever taken.

Until recent times, the English euthanasia society sought passage of a law that would allow only a rational adult, already dying in painful circumstances, to receive medical assistance in speeding up the process of death. No provision was made for ill persons unable to communicate their wishes, like those in a comatose condition.

In 1967, the British proposal was expanded to allow adults to sign a legally binding statement in advance of any illness, which would permit euthanasia to be administered under specific medical circumstances. The declaration provided for euthanasia "if I should at any time suffer from a serious physical illness or impairment reasonably thought in my case to be incurable and expected to cause me severe distress or render me incapable of rational existence."

In arguing for a euthanasia bill in the House of Commons in 1970, Labourite Dr. Hugh Gray said, "If I am involved in a motor accident on my way to the House and I suffer irreparable brain damage, I wish to be eased gently out of life. Call it suicide by proxy if you like—it is a choice which, as an adult, I should be able to make."

Dr. Gray said that the choice between life and death

47

should always be made by the individual himself. His values rather than the values of others should receive top consideration. At present, said Dr. Gray, the doctor makes all the decisions, and not always in accordance with the patient's wishes.

According to Dr. Gray, every person could sign the declaration stating whether he would be in favor of or opposed to euthanasia for himself under certain circumstances. The statement would then be attached to a person's medical record, readily available if situations arose where it might be applicable.

One of euthanasia's strongest advocates in the House of Lords has been Lord Raglan. He most recently introduced his own Voluntary Euthanasia Bill to the Lords in 1969, where it was rejected by a sixty-one to forty vote on its second reading. It would have authorized physicians to administer euthanasia to a patient suffering from irreparable physical injury. The patient would have been required to sign a statement requesting euthanasia under specified conditions, not less than thirty days before it would be administered.

The declaration which Lord Raglan proposed read:

I declare that I subscribe to the code set out under the following articles:

A. If I should at any time suffer from a serious physical illness or impairment reasonably thought in my case to be incurable and expected to cause me severe distress or render me incapable of rational existence, I request the administration of euthanasia at a time or in circumstances to be indicated or specified by me or, if it is apparent that I have become incapable of giving directions, at the discretion of the physician in charge of my case.

B. In the event of my suffering from any of the conditions specified above, I request that no active steps should be taken, and in particular that no resuscitatory techniques should be used to prolong my life or restore me to consciousness.

The bill also provided that the signer of the declaration had to be over the age of majority, and that two physicians would have to certify that the patient was in an incurable condition. Other sections of the bill declared that no doctor opposed in principle to euthanasia would be forced to participate in its administration, and that "no policy of insurance that has been in force for twelve months shall be vitiated by the administration of euthanasia to the insured."

A final clause of the bill stated that "terminal patients" would be entitled to the full amount of drugs needed to eliminate pain, and in cases "where severe distress cannot be alleviated by pain-killing drugs, the patient is entitled, if he so desires, to be made and kept entirely unconscious." The provisions of this clause would be available to all patients, even those who had not signed the euthanasia declaration.

In arguing for his bill, Raglan said that some people might be surprised that voluntary euthanasia was not already legal, since back in 1961 Parliament had enacted a law allowing a person to take his own life. "So it is not a question," he said, "of whether people should be given the right to kill themselves—this they already have; it is whether that liberty should be extended, under certain safeguards, to those dying people who are not in a position to help themselves and would like to have their lives terminated by the kindly action of medication administered by the agency of another."

He explained that the mail he had been receiving was ten to one in favor of his bill. However, he felt that since most of those who supported the measure were the old and the infirm, this bloc of support was by its nature not very vocal.

In his speech to the Lords, Raglan said, "I think it is highly significant that for the first time, up and down the country, we are talking not only about the length of life, but about the quality of it too. This bill is a liberal and humanitarian measure for those who treasure for themselves the quality of life as much as its quantity."

One of Raglan's most enthusiastic supporters was one of his colleagues, Lord Ritchie-Calder, who said his own advocacy of the measure was based on a personal family experience. He recalled how two of his aunts sacrificed their own opportunity for a happy life by caring for their severely ill sister. Through a childhood illness, the sister had become a drooling, helpless being who needed to be watched twenty-four hours a day. She lived to be sixty years old.

Ritchie-Calder deplored the way that his two aunts felt obligated to sacrifice any meaningfulness that their own lives had in order to care for their sister. He suggested that before we arbitrarily decide to prolong all life as long as possible, we consider the dignity and quality of that life.

Lord Platt, a former president of the Royal College of Physicians, has also attempted to influence the British lawmakers to pass proeuthanasia legislation. Platt has publicly stated three situations in which he feels euthanasia is humane, justifiable, and ethical. The most obvious case, he says, is that in which a person has suffered permanent and irreversible brain damage, yet can still be kept "alive" through the use of cardiac pacemakers and breathing machines. In a panel discussion at the Royal Society of Medicine, Platt said, "In such cases, after every possible test has been done, and after full consideration, I think there is general agreement that there comes a time when the apparatus must be switched off."

The second situation outlined by Platt is that in which a

patient is suffering from a fatal disease, such as terminal cancer. If high dosages of pain-killing drugs have the additional effect of shortening the patient's life, Platt contends that this is justifiable.

The third circumstance is that of a terminally ill patient who decides to consume a fatal overdose of drugs to release himself from his painful condition. On such an occasion, Platt says the doctor should allow the patient to carry out such an action.

He also indicates that there should be legislation to allow a healthy person to sign a statement ordering that extraordinary medical techniques not be used on him if he should ever become incapable of voicing such sentiments. Such a statement would be invaluable in the case of "the severe stroke which renders the patient quite unable to speak, unable to attend to himself for the needs of nutrition or excretion, and unable to move in bed without assistance. A similar state of affairs can arise in terminal neurological disease."

Platt says a person should be able to request beforehand that, in the event he ever is in such a condition, a doctor be permitted to legally end his life. "The whole point of the bill is that you should be able to declare your wishes while you are still capable of expressing them," he says.

A totally separate euthanasia proposal has been suggested by Professor W. J. Dempster, a consultant in organ transplantation at a British hospital. Writing in the journal *Medical Tribune* (May 1968), Professor Dempster advocated that euthanasia of the hopeless respirator case be legalized so that transplantation of organs can be carried out realistically. He said that to keep a person in a suspended state of artificial life benefits neither the dying patient nor his relatives who are subjected to severe mental anguish.

Professor Dempster recommended that a law be enacted which specified that two neurologists—each from a different hospital—would have to agree that the patient was beyond help. The doctors' records and recommendations would be available for inspection by appropriate personnel.

Although admitting that switching off the respirator already occurs in hospitals today, Professor Dempster explained that it was by private arrangement only, without any legal sanction. The law must be changed, he said, in spite of strong opposition to such revisions. He wrote, "In readjusting our official ethics to meet the current scientific necessities, a section of the community will suffer moral and spiritual agony. This is inevitable, but some of us suffer agony as the law now stands."

Even the United Nations has been asked to amend its Declaration of Human Rights to include a provision to allow incurable sufferers to ask for voluntary euthanasia. Advocates of the amendment already point to other parts of the declaration, which they claim make a euthanasia amendment an obvious addition. Article Five of the declaration, they say, already states that "No one shall be subjected to torture." But the United Nations has taken no action on the proposed amendment as yet.

Some attorneys believe that even without further legislative action, there may already be legal precedent in the United States for allowing a person to make his own life-and-death decisions. They refer to a case that came before the Illinois Supreme Court in 1965, which asserted the right of an individual to decline medical treatment for religious reasons, even if lack of care would cause death.

The case involved a Jehovah's Witness, who was in a Chicago hospital suffering from a peptic ulcer. She had told her doctor repeatedly for two years that she would refuse blood transfusions in accordance with the dictates of her religion. Her husband and two adult children agreed. She and her husband signed a statement stating their wishes, in order to relieve her doctor and the hospital of any civil liability that could ever result from a failure to administer the transfusions. But, despite this request and without notice to the patient or her family, her physician sought the appointment of a conservator who would agree to the blood transfusions.

The case eventually came before the state's high court, which ruled that since no minor children were involved, and since there was no clear and present danger to others, the court could not force a person to reject his own religious principles, despite the likelihood of hastening his own death.

The Illinois court said:

> Applying the constitutional guarantees and the interpretations thereof . . . to the facts before us we find a competent adult who has steadfastly maintained her belief that acceptance of a blood transfusion is a violation of the law of God. Knowing full well the hazards involved, she has firmly opposed acceptance of such transfusions, notifying the doctor and hospital of her convictions and desires, and executing documents releasing both the doctor and the hospital from any civil liability which might be thought to result from a failure on the part of either to administer such transfusions. No minor children are involved. No overt or affirmative act of appellant's offers any clear and present danger to society—we have only a governmental agency compelling conduct offensive to appellant's religious principles. Even though we may consider appellant's beliefs unwise, foolish or ridiculous, in the absence of an overriding danger to society we may not permit interference therewith in the form of a conservatorship established in the waning hours of her life for the sole purpose of compelling her to accept medical treatment forbidden

by her religious principles, and previously refused by her with full knowledge of the probable consequences. In the final analysis, what has happened here involves a judicial attempt to decide what course of action is best for a particular individual, notwithstanding that individual's contrary views based upon religious convictions. Such action cannot be constitutionally countenanced.

Since this court ruling, lawyers have speculated that since a person cannot be forced to accept medical treatment for religious reasons, then all individuals should be guaranteed the same right under the equal protection clause, even when religious issues are not involved.

A decision similar to the Illinois case was reached by a New York court where, for religious reasons, a patient refused blood transfusions as part of an operation. Although the hospital contended that the patient's refusal was analogous to suicide and thus prohibited by penal laws, the court ruled that "it is the individual who is the subject of a medical decision who has the final say" and that "this must necessarily be so in a system of government which gives the greatest possible protection to the individual in the furtherance of his own desires." Since the patient was mentally competent, he was ruled justified in disallowing the transfusions.

But despite these New York and Illinois rulings, euthanasia advocates are not satisfied to leave these life-and-death decisions to the interpretations of the courts. For until legislators act positively with binding statutes, the courts will continue to interpret the existing laws in the unpredictable way that they now are doing.

The anti-euthanasia laws themselves have been interpreted rigidly at times. But, just as often, there has been a gap between the law in theory and the law in actual usage. Grand juries and district attorneys have frequently failed to press charges against someone who may have obviously committed premeditated euthanasia. Juries have sometimes declined to convict the unmistakably guilty, and judges have reduced guilty sentences to a minimum.

In 1971, a seventy-nine-year-old man, kept alive by only a pacemaker, needed new batteries installed in the mechanism to keep it functioning. His wife objected, saying, "He is turning into a vegetable; isn't death better?" New York City's Cornell Medical Center, where the man was a patient, disagreed, and went to court to seek an overruling of the wife's wishes. The state supreme court, in declaring the ill man mentally incompetent, ruled that the hospital doctor should assume legal guardianship over the patient "to protect and sustain" his life. Shortly thereafter, the new batteries were installed.

Another court made a completely different decision in a case that developed in Milwaukee. In 1972, seventy-seven-year-old Gertrude Raasch had undergone two major operations for gangrene of the legs, in which parts of her limbs were amputated. Her doctors told her that a third operation would be necessary if she was to survive, but the patient refused to sign another surgical consent form. The hospital attempted to have her ruled mentally incompetent, and the case came before a county judge.

"There is absolutely no evidence of incompetence," ruled the court, "except that she is too weak to talk. . . . There is no question in my mind that Mrs. Raasch knew what she was being asked and she did not want the operation. I'm positive we're doing the right thing—we will leave Mrs. Raasch to depart in God's own peace. It is not the prerogative of this court to make decisions for adult, competent citizens, even decisions relating to life and death."

Mrs. Raasch died six weeks later.

4. The Medical Aspects of Euthanasia

Regardless of court decisions and any future changes in the law—and despite the reality that euthanasia is now being practiced furtively by some physicians—most doctors insist publicly that they will always remain opposed to it.

As one doctor says, "Euthanasia, whether it's legal or not, clashes directly with the Hippocratic Oath, which every doctor is bound by."

Under the Hippocratic Oath, physicians are obligated to both preserve life and relieve suffering. However, some doctors and theologians see a contradiction in these dual responsibilities. If prolonging the life of a dying patient causes him great physical and mental suffering, should the doctor still feel bound to postpone death as long as possible?

For example, consider the case of a patient with inoperable cancer of the throat. For months he has been in pain which drugs cannot completely control, and his difficulty in swallowing even liquids increases with time. Eventually, the cancerous growth spreads to his windpipe and larynx, making both speaking and breathing arduous tasks. His suffering is so great that he prays to be allowed to die. Which part of the Hippocratic Oath has precedence here: the relief of suffering or the preservation of life?

Without clearly confronting this knotty dilemma, the American Medical Association and the British Medical Association are opposed to all types of euthanasia. The Council of the World Medical Association also condemned the practice as far back as 1950. Its dictum against euthanasia reads:

> Whereas, the Council of the World Medical Association believes that the practice of euthanasia is contrary to public interest and to medical ethical principles as well as to natural and civil rights, and
> Whereas, such practice is contrary to the spirit of the Declaration of Geneva, therefore
> Be it resolved that the Council of the World Medical Association in session at Copenhagen, Denmark, April 24 to 28, 1950, recommends to the national medical associations that they condemn the practice of euthanasia under any circumstance.

One physician explains it this way: "I reject euthanasia—killing people is not what doctors should, or could, do."

But the strongest advocates of euthanasia—like the euthanasia societies in England and America—do not view their own proposals as supporting the "killing" of people. The societies favor only a voluntary euthanasia, which they see as *relieving* doctors of the responsibility of the life-or-death decision. If he so chooses, a doctor could have absolutely nothing to do with the entire euthanasia proceedings, much like the way no Catholic doctor is forced to perform an abortion under Britain's Medicare program. But, says a spokesman for the English euthanasia group, "When some poor devil is dying slowly . . . to dictate to him whether or not he has a moral right to release is impertinence."

At the 1969 meeting of the Second Euthanasia Conference, several doctors spoke on the issue of the Hippocratic Oath. Dr. Robert S. Schwab, professor of neurology at the Harvard Medical School, said, "One of the implications of the Oath is that you do things to help the patient. . . . What is meant is, do all you can that is GOOD for the patient. And when a patient is obviously, hopelessly dying—when to a physician with all his training there isn't any doubt—for him, then, to use measures that can't possibly do this man any good is, I think, malpractice and a violation of the Oath."

At the Euthanasia Conference a year earlier, in 1968, the Hippocratic Oath was discussed by Robert B. Reeves, Jr., chaplain of Presbyterian Hospital in New York. Chaplain Reeves said that "as long as medicine does observe [the Oath], I think we ought to be clear as to what it actually says. It does not say anything about the absolute value of life, biological continuance. 'So far as power and discernment shall be mine,' the Oath declares, 'I will carry out regimen for the benefit of the sick and will keep them from harm and wrong. I will give no deadly drug.'

"This provision, by the way, was aimed specifically at conspiracy, so that physicians would not enter into drug killing, which was rather a popular practice in political battles in that day. We have somehow got on to a vitalistic tack that has made simple biological continuance the absolute good."

But despite these appeals, many doctors still feel obligated to use every life-sustaining method available to them. "I've just seen and heard about too many miracle recoveries to ever pull the plug myself," says a San Diego physician. "There's just no way to explain the way some patients have come back after they've been given up for dead. Each day that you prolong life, you're giving the body's natural recovery processes a chance to work.

"We're also faced with the prospect of a wrong diagnosis when you have the human element involved," he continues. "And the way medical science is progressing, you just never know when a cure is going to be found for a terminal disease—or, even if not a cure, at least a drug or a treatment to give a patient a year or two more of life."

So in hospitals everywhere, long after death would have naturally come, machines keep hearts beating, lungs breathing, and kidneys performing. Since the body is kept functioning long past the time it would have otherwise died, killer growths like cancer spread farther than they otherwise would have, leaving even more of the body weak and deteriorated. Many more patients lose consciousness before they die today, as their bodies surrender long before their doctors do.

Frequently, even the sincerest motives of doctors to prolong life seem senseless under the prevailing circumstances. Not long ago, a physician was admitted to a hospital suffering from advanced cancer of the stomach. The patient was informed of the diagnosis and fully comprehended its implications. Although he was given large doses of pain-killing drugs, he still was racked with severe pain caused by the pressure of tumor deposits upon his spinal nerves.

The patient was operated upon, and surgeons discovered that the cancer had by this time spread to the liver. Another operation followed for removal of the stomach. Ten days after the second surgery, the patient collapsed from a clot in his lung artery. He was immediately operated on again, and the clot was successfully removed.

When the patient regained enough strength to talk to his doctors, he thanked them for their unfaltering dedication. But at the same time, he said that if he should collapse again, he wanted to be allowed to die. He said that the pain from the cancer had reached a level that he could no longer bear.

Less than two weeks later, he suffered a massive heart attack. But despite his stated wishes, he was revived by the hospital's resuscitation team. Four more times during the night, his heart stopped, and each time it was restarted. The body recovered enough to cling to life for three more weeks.

During the patient's final days, doctors could do nothing to stop his convulsions and violent vomiting. They were forced to begin intravenous feeding and blood transfusions. A tracheotomy was performed to ensure a clear air passage, but this was soon complicated when pneumonia set in. Massive doses of antibiotics were administered to combat the pneumonia. When the patient's own respiratory center was about to give out, an artificial respirator was being prepared to replace it. But before it could be installed, the patient's heart stopped for the last time. He was finally dead.

An Iowa housewife whose eighty-five-year-old father recently died from a prolonged and agonizing illness wonders whether some of our medical advances can really be called "progress." She says that for the last eighteen months of her father's life, he was less than human. "It is the most heart-breaking experience a human being can have, to watch a big proud man exist for months and months as a vegetable, being cared for as a baby."

She continues, "Yes, we have been given fabulous medical advances, but we have also been given brains to use it for the good of society—not to burden us as is being done. We are being crushed mentally, physically, emotionally, and financially.

61

"When we were created we were given a release—when you no longer could function and were flat on your back, you had pneumonia. Today you can't have an easy death. You die just one vein at a time."

One doctor who supports a liberalization of the euthanasia laws says that he realized the futility of needlessly prolonging life just a month after he graduated from medical school. Dr. Walter C. Alvarez of Chicago became an advocate of euthanasia while interning at a hospital in San Francisco. "I treated many poor people who had incurable cancer or kidney diseases that couldn't be helped," he recalls. "I had experience with several old men who told me, 'Don't keep me alive, doctor. What good will it do?'

"One fellow had tuberculosis which had attacked his larynx. Every cough gave him great pain. One night I gave him some medication, and the next day he told me he didn't want any more of it. He told me he had nothing to look forward to, and he didn't want to have to die all over again.

"It didn't take long for me to learn the unwisdom of keeping someone alive who had no hope in living."

Dr. Alvarez also remembers a case that involved one of his relatives, well into her sixties. She had a massive stroke, and although she was still able to speak and move part of her paralyzed body, her badly scarred brain had left her in a constant state of misery. "She lived for two or three more years," he says, "and during that agonizing period, she frequently asked me, 'How much longer will this have to go on?' She finally had another stroke that killed her, and I was relieved that her suffering had ended at last. If I could have somehow brought her back to her life of suffering, I don't think I would have done it. She would have been very unhappy if I had."

However, the ordeal of dying is constantly being prolonged

by thousands of doctors each day. Most hospitals have special teams to deal with crises like cardiac arrests. A nurse at a California hospital associated with a major medical school says that patients there rarely die a calm death. "Many of the doctors are young and they're just learning," she explains. "They'll use cardiac resuscitation in every conceivable situation, no matter how unreasonable it seems, even when a patient is beyond all hope. Sometimes they'll tell me they just did it for the learning experience.

"But when an old person is dying from cancer and has nothing more to look forward to than days or weeks of pain, why prolong the agony? Some people should just be allowed to die. There comes a time when a doctor should stop trying to prove his expertise, and start considering some of the human factors as well."

Dr. Roland Stevens, clinical associate professor of surgery and senior associate surgeon at the University of Rochester Medical School and Strong Medical Hospital, agrees that physicians sometimes view their own role in the death process unrealistically. "The average person seldom deals with death more than a few measured and memorable times in his life," he says. "Physicians, however, play a conspicuously active role in the dying process. They are seen by others and see themselves as champions chosen for the one purpose of preserving life. Insidiously, the promotion of the image becomes so sacred that when death occurs, the doctor feels a sense of guilt and defeat . . . an unreasoned, gut-feeling that his professional acumen was not what it should have been."

Consequently, says Dr. Stevens, an inexcusable method of treating grievously ill people is often adopted in hospitals. "Under the name 'intensive care,' a small crowd of highly competent specialists, each with his supporting team of technicians, shares the control of a patient's destiny—without anyone running the Department of Human Consideration. When a specialist's specific assignment is to revive a failing heart, he will surely continue applying every trick he knows until there are no more. So it goes with the failing kidney, liver or lung. This has led to some therapeutic endeavors, some financial commitments which can only be described as more heroic than humane."

Thus, there occur cases like a recent one involving a sixty-year-old man. He lay terminally ill in a hospital with cancer of the lung. The cancer soon invaded his brain and it was doubtful that he would live more than a few days. In the late evening, a nurse noticed that he had stopped breathing. The emergency resuscitation team was summoned, and the heart was started again. The patient was once again breathing on his own, and his heart was pumping blood. But the cancer was still there. Seven days later, the patient died. The additional week of life was nothing more than additional suffering for both the patient and his family.

Some psychiatrists speculate that doctors tend to have a high degree of thanatophobia (fear of death), which could help explain why they so often resort to extraordinary lifesaving measures for their patients. Dr. Herman Feifel, psychologist at the Los Angeles Veterans Hospital, has suggested that the reason an individual decides to become a doctor is often because of his high anxiety about death during his own childhood.

These opinions were supported by a 1967 study at the University of Southern California, which concluded that the fear of death was an important psychological reason why some people chose medical careers. Eighty-one physicians participated in the study, including twenty-nine interns, twenty-seven psychiatrists, and twenty-five surgeons. The results showed that the doctors "were significantly more afraid of death than both the physically sick and healthy normal groups.''

Medical schools have been blamed for not attempting to lessen these death fears, and for not helping doctors deal with the aging and the death of their patients more realistically. Medical training seldom confronts the unique problems of the aged straightforwardly, if at all.

Dr. Joseph T. Freeman conducted a study for the Senate Special Committee on Aging. He found that only fifty-one out of ninety-nine medical schools in the survey made any reference at all to aging in their 1969-70 catalogs. Only twenty-two of those schools offered specific clinical courses in aging as part of their general curriculum.

In a 1969 study sponsored by the Euthanasia Educational Fund, seventeen out of nineteen medical schools surveyed had no courses in their curriculum that dealt with death and dying. Seven of the schools had some type of course on dealing with terminal patients, but these were almost all courses in the psychiatry clerkship.

Dr. Charles H. Goodrich, an associate professor of community medicine at Mt. Sinai Hospital in New York, believes that medical education has failed completely in this area. At the First Euthanasia Conference in New York in 1968, he said, "We, unfortunately, are teaching about life or the erotic center of life. Sex is coming into the curriculum. But there are specific aggressive measures that are taken, not only not to teach but to repress any attempt to deal with the subject of death.

"The average medical student in this country comes from a family in the middle or upper-middle class. He has probably lived a sheltered life in regard to death, questions of death, certain physical representations of death, and frequently he enters the medical school with the idealistic notion that what he wants to do is to help people. And the first thing he is presented with is a cadaver, a dead body. Now, that should be the beginning of his education about death. Yet I don't know of any medical school, with the exception of some isolated experiments, which has on any concerted basis tried to deal with the first contact with death.

"Those of you who have seen a cadaver that has been in cold storage for months will understand that this student not only unlearns any feelings he may have about death, but represses them rapidly. He usually assigns a cadaver a nickname to permit him to deal with it as a thing rather than as a person. His repressed feelings come out as a kind of gallows humor usual among medical students.

"This inadequate training for death is then reinforced," continued Dr. Goodrich. "In the second year the student has his first encounter with the autopsy, where the patient has so recently died that it's hard to deny he was a person. The only help in terms of his feelings is being taught to concentrate his attention upon the organs rather than the person.

"By the time he gets to his clinical training and for the third time he sees the human body being assaulted by the knife on the surgical table, it is not surprising that he is detached from it as having anything to do with human life or death. The best we can say is that we have tried to train him in something called detached concern."

This frequent inability of doctors to relate to death on the human level has produced many distressing confrontations not only with dying patients, but with their families, too. Dr. Elisabeth Kubler-Ross found dozens of such instances in her extensive studies of death, which served as the basis for her book, *On Death and Dying* (1969). She conducted seminars at the University of Chicago Hospital with dying patients and their relatives.

A woman at Dr. Kubler-Ross's seminar related the story of her daughter, who had been sick with an undiagnosed illness. The child was hospitalized with fainting spells and a loss of appetite, but doctors expressed hopes that the illness was not serious. The woman and her husband visited their daughter in the hospital each day, but on a Tuesday when he had a cold, she went alone. That afternoon, a young doctor took her aside and directed her to a small isolated room. Before she could sit down, he blurted out, "Well, she has aplastic anemia and she's not going to get well, that's all."

The doctor proceeded to tell her, "Nothing can be done, we don't know the cause, we don't know the cure."

The mother, although staggered by the physician's words, was able to ask if the child would live much longer, at least maybe a year.

"Oh no, goodness, no," he replied matter-of-factly. Then he added, "There's a lot of people who have it, it's incurable and that's all there is to it. She'll just have to accept it."

When the woman spoke in front of Dr. Kubler-Ross's seminar, she said that "it was quite a shock the way it was presented to me and the fact that I was alone. If he had had me sit down at least and tell me, I think I could have accepted it a little bit better. . . . He could have told it to us frankly, but had a little bit of compassion and needn't seem so hard-hearted. I mean, how he put it, 'Well, you're not the only one in the world.' "

Will such doctors someday realize that a compassionate view of death is just as important as the technical lifesaving skills they have learned? Or will we go on having cases like a recent one involving an eighty-four-year-old man dying of cancer? The elderly patient had lost over fifty pounds as the cancer gradually decayed his body. The pains in his bones were severe and doctors began radiotherapy treatment, although aware there was no chance they could cure the disease. A day after the treatments began, the man suffered a massive bowel hemorrhage and he lapsed into unconsciousness. He was immediately transfused with five pints of blood, revived, and given his radiotherapy. Shortly thereafter, he was released from the hospital and was sent home to endure four more months of pain and deterioration before he died.

Some doctors are now beginning to question this widely accepted practice of keeping a dying patient alive at all cost. Dr. W. N. Hubbard, dean of the University of Michigan Medical School, has defended the right of a patient to die. At a graduation address at Albany Medical College, Dr. Hubbard warned that doctors must come to terms with the moral crisis of keeping the hopelessly ill alive. "To sacrifice human dignity at the time of death," he said, "or to make the process of dying a burden upon the living is not in the highest tradition of medicine, nor is it justified in the humanist traditions."

Dr. Hubbard also cautioned his audience, "The physician must beware of treating [primarily] his own anxiety that death represents his personal failure, by unrestrained use of life-support systems. . . . The human physician must learn to understand and accept death as an inevitable part of living."

Dr. Cicely Saunders, the British physician, says that a stage is reached when treatment becomes a care of the dying, and not the living. She believes there comes a time when the prolongation of life ceases to be in the best interest of both patient and doctor.

In an essay in *Death and Dying* (1969), Dr. Saunders writes, "Because something is possible does not mean that it is necessarily either right or kind to do it. One often sees a great weariness with the sort of pain and illness that brings our patients to us such as that of Sir William Osler who, when he was dying, said, 'I'm too far across the river now to want to come back and have it all over again.' I do not think he would have given a 'thank you' to someone who pulled him back at that stage. Recognition of this stage is not defeatism either on the part of the patient or on that of the doctor. Rather, it is respect and awareness of the individual person and his dignity."

Sometimes it takes the hard reality of one's own dying for doctors to face up to the human side of dying and euthanasia. The American physician Dr. Charlotte Perkins Gilman displayed a strong advocacy for voluntary euthanasia as she was dying of cancer. Before her death, she wrote, "No grief, no pain, misfortune or 'broken heart' is excuse for cutting off one's life while any power of service remains. But when all usefulness is over, when one is assured of an imminent and unavoidable death, it is the simplest of human rights to choose a quick and easy death in place of a slow and horrible one. Public opinion is changing on this subject. The time is approaching when we shall consider it abhorrent to our civilization to allow a human being to lie in prolonged agony which we should mercifully end in any other creature. Believing this choice to be of social service in promoting wider views on this question, I have preferred chloroform to cancer."

Some doctors say that their aversion to euthanasia stems from a fear of malpractice suits. Doctors are already paying up to $5,000 a year on malpractice insurance. And as one physician says, "Oftentimes relatives see a chance to make good on the death of a loved one by suing the doctor. If you give them even the slightest indication that you've gone a little bit out of the norm, you've laid yourself open for a suit."

Dr. Walter C. Alvarez remembers one instance in which he was threatened with a malpractice suit. One of his patients was suffering from terminal cancer which had grown into his spinal cord, causing great pain down his legs. One day the patient asked Dr. Alvarez to give him a bottle of morphine tablets, so that if the pain became unbearable during the night, he could escape from his misery by consuming the entire bottle.

"I gave him the bottle," says Dr. Alvarez, "but his wife found them and confiscated them. The man then begged me to get him another bottle and I did, but once again his wife found them. She confronted me with them and told me that she could have me put in jail for ten years for what I had done. I checked with an attorney and found out that she was right: I had technically broken the law."

However, there has been only a small number of malpractice cases involving euthanasia in the United States, and none of them has ended in a verdict of guilty of murder against the physician. Most lawyers agree that, if a doctor acts in accordance with the wishes of his patient and lets the patient die, it is very unlikely the doctor will he held liable. And even in a case of active euthanasia, judges and juries tend to show sympathy for the physician.

The most famous American case involving an instance of alleged active euthanasia occurred in New Hampshire in 1950. A general practitioner, Dr. Herman Sander, had dictated into the hospital record that he had injected air four times into the veins of an incurably ill patient, and that "she expired ten minutes after this started." Dr. Sander was accused of killing the fifty-nine-year-old woman, who had been dying of cancer. The charge was first-degree murder, punishable by life imprisonment.

During the trial, Dr. Sander contended that the patient's husband had endlessly pleaded with him to do something to end his wife's suffering. Indeed, the day before her death, the woman had been given strong doses of pain-killing drugs without any apparent effect.

Dr. Sander freely admitted injecting air into the patient, but he claimed that this action did not cause the death of the woman. A special nurse had found the patient unconscious and convulsing, with her extremities cold. No pulse was detected. Dr. Sander then injected the air with a sterile syringe. At the trial, he said he committed the action to ensure that she would suffer no more pain. He made the notation into the hospital record because he felt that all treatment should be registered by the attending physician.

The autopsy report attributed the patient's death to either cancer, starvation, bronchial pneumonia, or a combination of those—but not to air embolism. The report said that the blood clots in the brain indicated that death was gradual over a period of hours, rather than instantaneous. It further stated that at least forty cc. of air would be necessary to kill a human being, and Dr. Sander had only injected twenty to twenty-eight cc.

The family of the patient split during the trial: the husband and one brother supported the actions of the doctor, while another brother said that his sister's fate "should have been left to the will of God."

The community overwhelmingly supported Dr. Sander. A petition of support, signed by more than 90 percent of the registered voters in the town, described the physician as "a man of Christian virtue who has been devoted to the highest interests of human welfare at all times."

The jury (composed of nine Roman Catholics and three Protestants) acquitted Dr. Sander, claiming that the prosecution had failed to prove the doctor had caused the patient's death. However, shortly after the court decision, the state revoked Dr. Sander's license to practice medicine, and he was expelled from his county medical society. Three hospitals banned him from their staffs, and the American Academy of General Practice removed him from its membership rolls. It took court action on the doctor's part to regain his right to practice medicine.

Another case, this time in Sweden, involved a physician who had frequently questioned in his own mind the validity of keeping a patient alive when all hope was gone. He faced up to the issue when an eighty-year-old woman who had suffered a cerebral hemorrhage was being kept alive in a coma for weeks by intravenous feeding. He realized the futility of prolonging the woman's life, and received permission from her relatives to discontinue the intravenous treatment. The woman died shortly thereafter.

The state subsequently charged the doctor with contributing to the death of the elderly woman, although he contended that he had just "let her die peacefully." In his own defense, he pointed to an official statement to which all Swedish physicians are bound, which proclaims that "every patient is entitled to the treatment *which his condition requires,* and which is in accordance with medical science and proven experience."

The court eventually acquitted the physician, concluding that the woman was already dying and all reasonable hope for her recovery was gone. Under such circumstances, the court ruled that no further efforts to prolong life were required, and a cessation of previous treatment was considered justifiable.

The same physician soon found himself in court again with regard to his treatment of another patient—a sixty-five-year-old woman in a diabetic coma. In this case, the doctor had once again decided that the patient's condition was hopeless, and he sought permission from the next of kin to cease all life-sustaining treatment. It was not granted. In accordance with the family's wishes, he continued to keep the patient alive, but he still soon found himself the center of a legal controversy. The son of the patient accused the doctor of planning to murder his mother. The Swedish Central Medical Board charged the doctor with neglect and found him guilty. However, the courts overruled the judgment, deciding that the doctor had acted properly.

A later case in Sweden involved a well-known surgeon, Dr. Clarence C. Crafoord of the Karolinska Institute. In 1966, he removed a kidney from a woman dying of irreparable brain damage, and transplated the organ into a patient with serious kidney disease. The woman's husband had consented to the operation, and no legal charges were brought against Dr. Crafoord. However, his actions touched off a controversy in the nation's newspapers.

Dr. Crafoord firmly contended that the surgery was justified. He said that the donor had suffered a cerebral hemorrhage and she had been brought to the hospital in a comatose state. Her condition was deemed hopeless.

A decision had previously been made by the hospital staff, said Dr. Crafoord, that in cases of irreparable damage to the central nervous system, transplantation would be considered *before* legal death had occurred. He said that to postpone the operation until after death would greatly decrease the chances for a successful transplant.

In this controversial 1966 case, the operation began before circulation or respiration had ceased. Doctors admitted that mechanical devices could have been used indefinitely to keep the donor's body functioning, but that brain damage left no hope of recovery.

"A surgeon must feel that it is not his duty to give help to a person whose brain does not function," according to Dr.

Crafoord. "You are dead when your brain doesn't function, not when your heart has stopped beating. When the electrical activity of one's brain stops, as determined by electronic measurements, life is gone, and what is left is only a surviving organism which can be used to save the lives of other people who have diseases that are repairable."

It's difficult to know exactly how frequently euthanasia is being practiced quietly and without publicity. When questioned face-to-face, most physicians will deny ever considering euthanasia. And many private surveys indicate similar sentiments.

But in a few isolated polls, the results have been far different. At a medical meeting in the Midwest in the early 1960s, the doctors in the audience were asked to raise their hands only if they had never practiced euthanasia. Not a hand was raised.

In his 1971 president's address before the Association of American Physicians (AAP), Dr. Robert H. Williams reported the responses to a questionnaire submitted to members of the AAP and the Association of Professors of Medicine. According to Dr. Williams, 87 percent of the doctors who returned the questionnaire indicated they were in favor of passive euthanasia, and 80 percent said they had used it at least once in their practice. Only 15 percent said they favored active euthanasia.

In an earlier poll conducted in October 1962, the periodical *New Medical Materia* surveyed medical opinion in all parts of the country. Its results showed 31.2 percent of the doctors questioned believed there was justification for euthanasia for patients who were hopelessly and terminally ill. A slightly higher number (32.9 percent) said euthanasia was warranted in the case of an infant born with irreparable birth defects and no chance of a normal life.

74

One doctor, a California physician, says he has practiced euthanasia just once. "It involved a patient who was dying of leukemia," he recalls. "It was near the end, and blood transfusions were being given to keep her alive. She was suffering terribly with abscesses that had formed. Finally, I just decided to let her die. Maybe if we had continued the transfusions, we could have kept her alive for another few days. But it just would have meant more torment for her and her family."

Dr. Eliot Slater of the psychiatric genetics unit of London's Maudsley Hospital has said that when all that doctors can do in certain cases is to slow up the process of dying, they are working against nature. Speaking to a suicide prevention conference in 1969, he remarked that if incapacities become overburdening, death is often preferable to life.

According to Dr. Slater, physicians should not consider it a duty to always prolong the end of a patient's life. "This simple-minded view was, perhaps, a fair one in times gone by, but even now there are cases in which it is dangerously irrelevant and more and more calls for reconsideration."

He noted that the death of Socrates is the ideal upon which many terminally ill patients wish to model their own dying. "Yet what can the sufferer do to attain his end?" he asked. "There exists for him no automated Euthanasia Institute, and he cannot call on his doctor or family or his friends to murder him."

When there is no chance to return a patient to a healthy condition, Dr. Slater believes that retarding the dying process only increases the length of the illness and thus of the suffering, too. "Long illness is only to be endured if there is a hope of eventual recovery," he said. "It should not be endured when there is no such hope."

Dr. Slater contends that when a patient requests the right to die, no one can stand in his way. "A man's life is his own,

75

and if we say it is not, we are saying that he is a slave and not a free man. Slavery is still slavery, even when it is the near and dear ones who are the slavemasters."

Writing in the *Journal of the American Medical Association* (September 29, 1962), Dr. Frank J. Ayd, chief of psychiatry at Baltimore's Franklin Square Hospital, said, "When death is imminent and inevitable, it is neither scientific or humane to use artificial life-sustainers to protract the life of a patient. Instead when a realistic hope of recovery has evaporated, it is the right of the patient to choose only ordinary means to sustain his life and it is the duty of the doctor to provide palliative care. Only when there is a reasonable hope of sustaining life for several weeks or months, and if during this time the patient can be comfortable, should we exert every effort to delay death. Otherwise life-preserving treatment ceases to be a gift and becomes instead, a scientific weapon for the prolongation of agony. As physicians we must recognize the dignity of man and his right to live and die peacefully."

But apparently most physicians do not practice what Dr. Ayd advocates. Joseph Fletcher, a professor of social ethics and moral theology at the Episcopal Theological School in Cambridge, Massachusetts, believes that doctors rarely act mercifully with terminally ill patients. "The biggest obstacle to a compassionate and honest understanding of this problem is a superstitious concept of 'nature' inherited from an earlier, prescientific culture," he wrote in the October 1960 issue of *Harper's Magazine.* "People often feel that death should be 'natural'—that is, humanly uncontrolled and uncontrived. . . . For example, one doctor with an eighty-three-year-old patient, paralyzed by a stroke and a half-dozen other ailments, tells the compassionate family that he will do nothing, 'leave it to God.' But God does not cooperate; their mother goes on gasping. . . . For the fact is that medicine is an interference with nature. It freely cooperates with or counteracts and foils nature to fulfill humanly chosen ends."

The intensity of despair that a family feels during the lingering death of a loved one is reflected in this story related by a woman whose eighty-one-year-old uncle had died a few weeks earlier. "He had lived a full and complete life," she says. "Even after he retired, he kept active. He became an artist, and was able to capture with his brush some of the real beautiful things of life.

"When he had a massive cerebral, we were all grief-stricken. But when his doctor told us that he probably would die within a few hours without ever regaining consciousness, I guess I was a little relieved, too, knowing that he would at least die peacefully.

"I was naturally disturbed then when the doctor told us he had ordered 'heroic' methods to keep my uncle breathing and functioning, even if it was in a less than human state. The doctor appeared to be personally threatened when I asked him why he wouldn't let my uncle die. He told me, 'I'm no murderer, I'm a doctor.'

"My uncle lived for eleven more months. He never regained consciousness, and was alive in name only. Our whole family suffered terribly during the entire period, and by pooling our resources, we were barely able to pay the medical expenses.

"To use the doctor's word, sometimes I think 'murder' might be a little more humane than what all of us went through."

This family disruption caused by a prolonged illness was discussed by Sir George Pickering, Regius Professor of Medicine at Oxford University, in a January 18, 1968 article in *New Scientist.* Dr. Pickering, an advocate of "death with dignity," wrote, "I know of nothing more tragic than the disruption of a happy and productive family life by an ancient, bedridden, incontinent and confused parent or grandparent. What might have been a happy and respectful memory becomes a nightmare and a horror. I still recoil from the sight of old people being kept alive by a constant monitoring of their heartbeat and the team of nurses and doctors ready to pounce upon them when it stops. For my own part, when my time has come to die by natural causes, I hope I shall be allowed to do so."

When doctors refuse to release their patients from a prolonged and terminal illness, the patients and the families themselves sometimes, in desperation, carry out the actions they wanted their physicians to perform. In Pennsylvania, a seventy-one-year-old retired schoolteacher, who said she believed in mercy killings, admitted in court to helping her seventy-seven-year-old sister commit suicide. The older woman, who was terminally ill, had told her sister, "I cannot endure the pain any longer. I am going to take my own life." The younger sister told her that it was her life, and if ending it was what she wanted, she should do it. The ill woman swallowed some sleeping pills with the water that her sister brought her. Before she died, she said, "Now, I am going to my mother and a beautiful restful sleep."

A coroner's jury ordered that the surviving sister be held for trial on a homicide charge, but a judge dismissed the case.

In another case, a woman was admitted to a Chicago hospital in 1967, near death from an overdose of sleeping pills. She was suffering from leukemia, and had been in terrible pain for some time. During her second day in the hospital's intensive care unit, her twenty-four-year-old son kissed her and then fired three bullets through her head.

The victim's son, a college student, was charged with first-degree murder, but a jury found him not guilty by reason of temporary insanity.

The *Chicago Daily News* reported, "After a trial of one week, Robert Waskin was freed by a jury that deliberated only forty minutes before determining that he was temporarily insane when he shot his mother three times. The jury further found that he was no longer insane. The foreman of the jury commented: 'He knew he shot his mother. That was not disputed, but the prosecution failed to show he was of sound mind when he did it.' Robert Waskin is quoted as he prepared to pick up the threads of a nearly shattered life: 'The moral issue of euthanasia . . . was not taken up at the trial, and it should have been faced squarely. Someday it will have to be.' "

A well-publicized tragedy in 1965 involved sixty-one-year-old Mary Happer, a sister-in-law of the United States ambassador to South Vietnam, Maxwell Taylor. Miss Happer had a terminal stomach tumor, and being a Christian Scientist, she had refused medical treatment. She endured great pain, and those close to her suffered along with her.

One day, her best friend, onetime teaching colleague Dorothy Butts, visited her at a Christian Science convalescent home. The two ladies talked for a while, then went for a drive and returned about four o'clock, and went to Miss Happer's room. With the door closed, Miss Butts raised a .22-caliber revolver to her friend's head and pulled the trigger twice, killing her instantly.

As nurses rushed into the room, Miss Butts slipped away and drove to a police station. She parked her car there and used the gun once more, this time killing herself. Police found a note, which said, "Today, I killed my best friend,

Mary Happer, of 7305 River Road, Bethesda, Maryland. I had to let her find relief from the terrible pain that was killing her cruelly."

Following the disclosure of the facts surrounding the Happer case, one doctor asked, "Could this tragedy have been averted if euthanasia had been available to the ill woman? If the dying woman had a legal way to escape the pain, would that have prevented a single tragedy from becoming a double tragedy?"

Yet many doctors refuse to publicly support the legalization of even passive euthanasia. One of the strongest recent indictments of euthanasia by the medical profession came from a council of the British Medical Association which investigated the controversial issue in 1971. Dr. Ronald Gibson, a general practitioner and chairman of the eight-man council, said that even if a voluntary euthanasia bill were ever to become law, he would refuse to participate in such action. He also said that he was certain that 99 percent of his medical colleagues would agree with him. Doctors who would assist a patient to die would be nothing more than "murderers," he explained. According to the BMA council's report, the purpose of medicine is to heal and cure and to relieve suffering, not to serve as an executioner.

The Voluntary Euthanasia Society quickly countered the charges made in the British Medical Association's report. It contended that the investigating council was composed solely of physicians who already were strongly opposed to voluntary euthanasia, thus accounting for the report's strong bias. Members of the panel, therefore, were only searching out arguments supporting views they had already held.

The society refuted a claim by the BMA that euthanasia would put an intolerable added responsibility upon physicians. In reality, society spokesmen said, doctors are already constantly making life-and-death decisions—like deciding whether to operate on a very ill patient who might die during the operation. This is a responsibility which doctors are trained and educated to assume. The euthanasia society contended that doctors, like the rest of mankind, cannot escape from their life-and-death responsibilities.

The society also questioned the BMA's views that adequate safeguards for voluntary euthanasia would be impossible to enact. The BMA had expressed fears that once euthanasia became law, then its use could be seriously abused.

But the Voluntary Euthanasia Society pointed to two combined national opinion polls, each of which surveyed 1,000 general practitioners at random from the *Medical Register*. The doctors were asked, "If voluntary euthanasia were to be sanctioned by law in certain circumstances, do you think that appropriate safeguards (as simple as possible) could be devised?" Of those who replied, 44.3 percent answered yes and 43.5 percent, no.

The BMA report was also criticized for always considering death to be an unmitigated evil. The society argued that for a man hopelessly ill with a painful disease, death could be a welcome blessing. Similarly, the society doubted whether life was a good and desirable state for a person existing in a vegetable condition.

The euthanasia society also struck out at the BMA contention that dying persons do not wish to determine their own end. Rather, the society stated, most intelligent people would gladly welcome the opportunity to manage their last days. All men, the society said, should have this right of self-determination.

Some other questionable statements in the BMA report were also criticized. The BMA, for example, stated, "It seems an anachronism to introduce [euthanasia] at a time when capital punishment has been abolished and the young are openly moving toward pacifism." The euthanasia society argued that there was no relationship between capital punishment and euthanasia. And if the young were evolving into pacifists, it was probably because they were becoming more humanitarian and more concerned with human suffering. Thus, they would be more inclined to support humane euthanasia legislation.

Although many doctors still seem to stand firm in their opposition to euthanasia, others are slowly changing their minds. Chaplain Robert B. Reeves, Jr., of New York's Presbyterian Hospital is noticing some alteration of viewpoints. "I keep encountering physicians at our hospital," he says, "who are quite willing, if a person is in very bad shape, to say, 'Well, we're not going into any heroics—we will not institute treatment.' Other physicians will carry it a step further and interrupt treatment, if the case is hopeless. But few will go on to give massive doses of a drug whose result is almost bound to be fatal. Some do. Most tend to shy away. I think the religious conscience would go farther than the medical conscience at this point, feeling that though an indirect result of the administration of the drug might be to bring death, the relief to pain would take priority."

Some physicians are speaking out on the subject of euthanasia. When the Ciba Foundation brought together distinguished doctors and lawyers from both Europe and America, the president of the Swedish Society of Surgery, Dr. G. B. Giertz, asked the symposium: "Is it in fact intended that we shall provide the medical services with resources for furnishing life-supporting measures for every individual who might quality for it, even when the prospects of securing a recovery are negligible? Should we not accept that man shall decide what is fit for life and what is not, and direct our resources to the former?"

Dr. Giertz continued, "The thought that we physicians should be obliged to keep a patient alive with a respirator when there is no possibility of recovery, solely to try to prolong life by perhaps twenty-four hours, is a terrifying one. It must be regarded as a medical axiom that one should not be obliged in every situation to use all means to prolong life. . . . We refrain from treatment because it does not serve any purpose, because it is not in the patient's interest. I cannot regard this as killing by medical means: death has already won, despite the fight we have put up, and we must accept the fact."

American physicians are speaking out, too. In 1968, the new president of the American College of Surgeons told his constituency that doctors may sometimes have to consider euthanasia by omission of treatment in cases of the hopelessly ill. Dr. Preston Allen Wade of New York City said, "Advanced scientific methods of care of the elderly and those with far advanced diseases have posed new problems in this field. In many instances, the old, debilitated patient can be kept alive, sometimes indefinitely, and many are caused to live longer and often unhappily by constant and costly medical treatment."

A surgeon, according to Dr. Wade, "cannot sacrifice human dignity at the time of death if his treatment only prolongs the process of dying and adds to the suffering of the patient and his family."

A nurse in a Virginia hospital agrees, and she has given specific instructions to her family on the type of care she wishes to receive in a terminal illness. "I have seen too many old people with no hope, unconscious—fed through tubes and living on year after year with no chance of recovery," she says. "One woman lived three years while her old husband had to almost go bankrupt trying to pay the $900 a month nursing bill.

83

"I have written a letter concerning my wishes in this matter, and my husband knows where it is. I do not want to live if I have an accident or a stroke that leaves me mangled. Having tubes in and out of the body is not really living to me. I don't want my husband to spend all his money on me to keep a 'spark' of life alive."

Despite fears of legal reprisals, even a few doctors who have already practiced euthanasia are breaking their silence. An English physician, Dr. Maurice Millard, delivered a public speech in which he described how one of his patients, a devout Christian lady, asked him to administer a "fatal dose" of drugs if she ever fell victim to a painful and deadly disease. The woman later contracted incurable cancer, and after discussing it with her sister and brother-in-law, she asked the doctor to end her suffering with the drug dosage. A bedside service was held with relatives attending, and the doctor read a prayer. Then, acting out of compassion, he gave in to the woman's request and injected the drug.

Dr. Millard explained that he chose to tell the story publicly to offer dramatic proof of the need for legislation allowing a doctor and his patient to reach a mutual understanding in such circumstances.

England's euthanasia society publicly supported Dr. Millard, insisting that every doctor must be guided by his own conscience. However, many members of the medical profession disapproved of Dr. Millard's actions. Some doctors condemned the act by citing the passage of the Hippocratic Oath which states, "I will give no deadly medicine to anyone if asked, nor suggest any such counsel."

England's Medical Council refused to censure or penalize Dr. Millard unless the family of the victim complained—and they had consented to the euthanasia being performed. Law enforcement agencies were unable to indict him for the act because he would not reveal who the patient was, or where or when she died.

Dr. Walter Sackett of Florida is another physician who has publicly admitted to failing to prolong lives of terminal patients. "Most of the patients I have let die have been under my care for years," says Dr. Sackett. "I know what they would have wanted, and I know I'm doing the right thing."

One of Dr. Sackett's own sons died instantly in an automobile accident several years ago. And when he walks through the hospital accident wards today, Dr. Sackett sees patients who he thinks are far less lucky than his son—who have suffered such severe brain damage, they are actually "dead" except in the legal sense. He admits that if some of these severely injured patients were his own, he would recommend withholding antibiotics if they developed pneumonia, thus letting them die.

"When someone tells me I'm playing God in these instances, I wholeheartedly disagree with them," he says. "In fact, what I'm doing is letting God take over."

Dr. Sackett believes that medicine must concern itself more with the quality of life than with the quantity of life. There must be a change in our thinking, he says, to make the process of dying more comfortable and dignified.

According to Dr. Sackett, a single visit to a general hospital, a nursing home, or a state facility will offer proof of the swarm of bottles, tubes, resuscitators, respirators, and pacemakers that so often only prolong an inevitable death. "Witness, as I did," he says, "a patient eighty-five years old with a terminal blood condition, receiving three transfusions daily, to a total of sixty-five, even though six times during that period 'code four' (the emergency resuscitation call) was sounded on him before he was allowed to die. Imagine the emotional turmoil in that family, the economic bankruptcy of the individual and his family, as well as of all levels of government that could ensue from millions of such episodes."

Some doctors, tormented by the issues but still not willing to administer death-inducing drugs themselves, often resort to other alternatives. Some admit to placing a number of pills at the bedside of the patient. They will then advise the terminally ill person, "You are to take one pill every four hours. If you take them all at once, they will kill you." The decision is then left up to the patient.

A Colorado woman in her eighties wrote a letter to the *Denver Post* (April 1, 1967), pleading that she be allowed to have "one more pill" when death is near. "I want the pill in my possession—that's all—but early enough so that I may go out with decency and self-respect," she wrote. "You need only give me pain or sleeping pills with definite instructions of how many not to take, and you are free, and what it would mean to me is greater than all the Social Security the state can offer.

"No, I haven't overdrawn the picture. Eighty years is a nice length of time to have watched the change in seasons on our beautiful earth—to appreciate. Why wait until my eyes fail me and my senses grow so concerned over the pains and aches in the old body that I no longer see the beauty of the earth, which after all of this time, seems the one thing worth having lived for."

A housewife who has signed the Euthanasia Educational Fund's "living will" hopes that her own physician will avoid prolonging her life if she should ever become terminally ill. "I've explained the situation to both my doctor and the members of my family. They know that under no circumstances do I want extreme measures taken. I want to be made comfortable, but not to have my life needlessly prolonged.

86

"My grandfather spent the last six years of his life in a coma," she continues, "and he finally died when he was ninety. It was a tremendous financial and emotional burden on the entire family. It disrupted all of our lives, just to keep the heart beating of someone who was totally unaware of what was happening. The doctors said all along that he had no chance of recovery, but still he was kept going for years and years."

Changes may be inevitable as medical science's ability to prolong life—all types of life—continues to increase. Dr. Theodore Fox, in a 1965 speech to the Royal College of Physicians, summed up the physician's dilemma. He said that "though cures are getting commoner, so too are half-cures, in which death is averted but disability remains."

Dr. Fox explained that although it is a good rule that physicians should preserve life, there are times when following such a rule is not good medicine. "The doctor's overriding duty is to treat his neighbor as himself and this permits, indeed enjoins, occasional exceptions to other rules," he said. "More and more often we are able to prolong active lives that can never again have purpose or meaning, but the fact that something can be done does not mean that we are obliged to do it."

Dr. Roland Stevens of the University of Rochester Medical School believes that doctors must face the issue squarely. "Death is man's greatest blessing," he says, "when it cancels a life wracked with suffering and stripped of its meaning. The prolongation of suffering is not a compassionate act. We do not have it in our power many times to judge the end of tolerance in the lives of our patients and friends. We ought to have the courage to practice—and to preach compassion."

5. The Religious Aspects of Euthanasia

Religious teachings have always played a dominant role in discussions of euthanasia. The Western religions almost unanimously condemn active euthanasia, in which a doctor administers a fatal dosage of a drug to a hopelessly ill person. However, the churches are not nearly as strongly opposed to passive euthanasia, where the use of life-sustaining treatments are discontinued to allow the patient to die.

The Roman Catholic church has not wavered from its strict opposition to active euthanasia that dates back to the time of St. Augustine. At various times in its history, Catholicism has publicly condemned euthanasia through official church pronouncements. An official declaration from the Roman Holy Office states:

> The teaching of the Church is unequivocal that God is the supreme master of life and death and that no human being is allowed to usurp His dominion so as deliber-

ately to put an end to life, either his own or anyone else's without authorization . . . and the only authorizations the Church recognizes are a nation engaged in war, execution of criminals by a Government, killing in self defense. . . . The Church has never allowed and never will allow the killing of individuals on grounds of private expediency; for instance . . . putting an end to prolonged suffering or hopeless sickness . . .

In 1970, a convention of Roman Catholic physicians heard Pope Paul VI denounce euthanasia in a message that also condemned abortion and infanticide. "The influence of Christianity eradicated these barbarian methods little by little," the pontiff said, "but the materialistic concepts of a pagan eugenics tend to make the most wrongful practices respectable again."

He also emphasized that Christian anthropology observed "absolute respect for man, from the first moment of his conception to his last breath of life."

According to Pope Paul, "It is a temptation, in effect, to take the life of a man under the false pretext of giving him a pleasant and quiet death so as not to see him continue a hopeless life of atrocious agony. But without the consent of the sick person euthanasia is murder. His consent would make it suicide. Morally this is a crime which cannot become legal by any means."

Most Catholic scholars point to two major theological teachings to support their opposition to euthanasia. The first is a resolute belief in the sanctity of human life. "God created all of life," a Los Angeles priest recently told an audience of worshippers. "As the Creator, He is the only Master over it. Recognizing that human life is the work of God, it is man's duty to conserve that life."

Catholicism teaches that man is merely a "custodian of

life," just a steward over his own body, entrusted with the duty of preserving it. He has only "useful dominion" over his own body, and not "absolute dominion." Since a person does not in fact "own" his life, he does not have the prerogative of allowing a doctor to end it under any circumstances.

Even the liberal wing of the Catholic church has refused to waver from this traditional teaching opposing active euthanasia. The new Dutch catechism says that "it is wrong to put an end to life willfully—to kill those who are incurably ill physically or mentally (by euthanasia, for instance) or to commit suicide. Our life has been given us by God and we cannot end it as we will. The reason given for ending life is always that it has become meaningless and valueless. This can never be accepted by the Christian faith, which believes in every life, from the first moment of conception."

Roman Catholics also cite a belief in the meaningfulness of suffering as a second justification for opposing active euthanasia. "God is omnipotent," says one priest. "When there is suffering on this Earth, there is purpose for it happening. And since God possesses a far superior intellect to man, sometimes it is impossible for man to completely understand this purpose."

Suffering, according to the Roman Catholic position, instills humility in man, for he sees that in his time of suffering, God, and not man, can offer him comfort. Suffering, when it is accepted, "purifies" man, for he has relinquished himself to the will of God.

Protestantism approaches euthanasia from a wide range of viewpoints. Since the time of the Reformation, there has not been one single spokesman representing all of Protestant thinking. At one end of the spectrum are those who condemn active euthanasia as strongly as the Roman Catholic church, and usually for the same reasons: the sanctity of human life,

91

and the meaningfulness of suffering. Then there is a large body of Protestant thought which contends that each individual case should be weighed on its own merits, and the decision of whether or not to administer euthanasia should be left to the family and physician. There is also a group which believes that euthanasia is always warranted under certain circumstances, and that when a terminally ill patient requests it, the medical profession should be obligated to administer it.

There have been several prominent Protestant theologians in the forefront of the proeuthanasia movement. Among them are Reverend Leslie D. Weatherhead, a well-known Methodist minister, and Joseph Fletcher of the Episcopal Theological School. Other advocates have included a president of England's Free Church Council and a chairman of the Congregational Union. Even the archbishop of Canterbury admitted in 1936 that there are cases in which some means of shortening life may be justified.

Jewish teaching has dealt only infrequently with the subjects of euthanasia and death. Rabbi Immanuel Jacobovits writes in *Jewish Medical Ethics* (1959), "The predominantly 'this-worldly' character of Judaism is reflected in the relative sparsity of its regulations on the inevitable passage of man from life to death. The rabbis, as we have noted, place a severely practical emphasis on the axiom that the ordinances of God exist so that man 'shall live by them.'"

But much like Catholicism, Judaism universally condemns active euthanasia on the basis of the sanctity of human life. Jacobovits points out that the sacred book, the Torah, condemns euthanasia with the commandment "Thou shalt not kill." This Sixth Commandment, which is also an integral part of both Catholic and Protestant teachings, is cited by all the major religions in their arguments against euthanasia.

However, Judaism does not share the Catholic belief in the meaningfulness of suffering. In fact, Jewish teaching condemns suffering as a "curse," and maintains that there is no virtue in bodily pain.

Some doctors doubt just how devoted the truest believer is in the doctrine of purposeful suffering. "A lot of people claim that suffering may be good for their souls," says one physician, "but I haven't met too many of them who apply that to their own lives. It seems that as soon as a person feels the slightest amount of discomfort—even if it's just a headache—he's on the phone to his doctor, asking what he can take to stop the pain. And I have yet to meet anyone who has refused an anesthetic during an operation because the suffering would be good for him."

Other nontheologians have also attacked this "value of suffering" tenet. A. T. Welford, professor of psychology at the University of Adelaide in Australia, told a 1969 meeting of the Australian Medical Association, "Certainly some suffering is needed to bring out the best in any individual; for example, it is stunting to a child's mental and emotional development to protect it from all struggle, worry, pain and disappointment.

"It would be wrong, however, to conclude from this that all suffering brings gain," said Welford. "During the last twenty years, we have come to realize that stresses and anxieties can be beneficial in small doses, either intense for a short time or milder for a longer period, but can be devastating to both mental and physical integrity if intense and unremitting, especially if they do not point to a way of future escape. The sufferings engendered by the problems of life and death . . . are of this latter kind, and while they may occasionally yield rare moral insight, their effects are all too likely to be degrading rather than edifying."

93

Welford also directed his attention to the religious objection that euthanasia tampers with God's power. "It is true that some of man's tampering with nature has not been entirely fortunate in its results; but if all attempts to manipulate nature were disallowed, we should have to rule out not only agriculture, stock breeding and civil engineering, but also education and medicine—activities which the Church has traditionally fostered. In short, many tamperings with nature are good rather than bad in both their intentions and their effects, and represent working with rather than against God."

The use of the "Thou shalt not kill" commandment to justify opposition to euthanasia is also being questioned in many circles. Glanville Williams, the respected British attorney, in his book *The Sanctity of Life and the Criminal Law* (1957), says that the commandment has been interpreted incorrectly. Williams writes, "The true translation of the Sixth Commandment is not 'Thou shalt not kill,' but 'Thou shalt do no murder' as the *Book of Common Prayer* has it; and it is only by a stretch of words that a killing with the patient's consent, to relieve him of inexpressible suffering, can morally be described as murder. If wholesale killing in war and the punitive killing of criminals are not 'murder,' surely a killing done with the patient's consent and for his benefit as an act of mercy can claim to be excluded from this ugly word. . . . Even on the religious hypothesis of a soul, to release the soul from the tortured body and set it at liberty is surely to confer a benefit upon it and not an injury."

Dr. Edmund Leach expressed similar feelings in a television lecture on the British Broadcasting Company: "Our ordinary morality says that we must kill our neighbor if the state orders us to do so—that is to say, as a soldier in war or as an executioner in the course of his duty—but in every other case

94

we must try to save life. But what do we mean by that? Would a headless human trunk that was still breathing be alive? And if you think that is just a fanciful question, what about a body that has sustained irreparable brain damage but can still be kept functioning by the ingenuity of modern science?"

When the discussion of euthanasia moves from the active to the passive form, church teachings noticeably change. Most religious groups take a more lenient view of passive euthanasia. Robert B. Reeves, Jr., chaplain of New York City's Presbyterian Hospital, says, "Certainly I know of no moral grounds in any of the faiths that would argue against stopping treatment, or, indeed, not starting treatment, of a patient facing a miserable death, if that treatment merely served biological prolongation. If you moved from that to the administration of a drug that might bring death as a by-product, there might be more question."

Some religious leaders are even choosing passive euthanasia for themselves. Many have signed the Euthanasia Educational Fund's "living will." Others who have already died chose a peaceful death over a painful prolongation of a life they felt was useless.

A California physician relates the story of a seventy-year-old Episcopal bishop who was suffering through a terminal illness. The bishop was unable to swallow because of brain damage. "He asked me if he'd ever be able to swallow again," the doctor recalls. "I told him that he wouldn't, and that he would have to be fed with a tube. Then he said that if that was the case, he would want to die instead. After determining that that was really his wish, I gave him enough medication to ensure there would be no pain, and in five days he was dead."

Many theologians would not be opposed to such actions. The United States Catholic Conference, in its meeting in November 1971, condemned euthanasia. But in the same directive, it said, "The failure to supply the *ordinary* means of preserving life is equivalent to euthanasia. However, neither physician nor patient is obliged to use *extraordinary* means."

Pope Paul VI has agreed, explaining that while medicine is required to fight against death with all resources available, once that battle appears lost, it is not necessary that *all* survival techniques be used. He has said that it would just be "useless torture" to maintain a person in a vegetative state when his disease was terminal.

Almost two decades ago, Pope Pius XII spoke about the same issue. In a public speech, he said that real human life persists only as long as the body's vital functions continue to operate spontaneously, without the assistance of artificial techniques. When questioned as to whether an oxygen tent could be removed from an unconscious and dying patient when there was no hope for recovery and death was inevitable, he replied that it could. He found no objections to a relative asking doctors to desist "in order to permit the patient, already virtually dead, to pass on to peace."

In regard to resuscitating a patient who had stopped breathing, Pope Pius stated, "If it appears that the attempt at resuscitation constitutes in reality such a burden for the family that one cannot in all conscience impose it upon them, they can lawfully insist that the doctor should discontinue these attempts, and the doctor can lawfully comply."

Pope Pius also said that if the dying person is conscious, he should be free to choose whether or not his life should be prolonged. He said, "Morals evidently condemn mercy killing, that is, the intention to cause death. But if a dying person consents, it is permissible to use with moderation narcotics that will allay his suffering but will also cause quicker death."

The pontiff said, "If there exists no direct or casual link, either through the will of interested parties or by the nature of things, between the induced unconsciousness and the shortening of life—as would be the case if the suppression of the pain could be obtained only by the shortening of life; and if, on the other hand, the actual administration of drugs brings about two distinct effects, the one the relief of pain, the other the shortening of life, the action is lawful."

Another prominent Roman Catholic theologian, the Most Reverend Fulton J. Sheen of New York, also believes that physicians are not morally obligated to indefinitely prolong the lives of hopelessly ill and suffering patients. "If the doctor told me," he says, "that extraordinary means would be needed and I was lying with a body full of tubes to keep me alive, I would ask him to take them out. I find no moral difficulty in this."

Bishop Sheen contends that doctors are not obligated to keep patients alive using means such as oxygen tents and intravenous feeding. The family, he says, should follow the advice of their doctor in cases where "extraordinary" techniques are needed to keep a patient alive.

The Protestant orders have generally agreed to the use of passive euthanasia, too. Joseph Fletcher, the minister and professor at the Episcopal Theological School, was one of the earliest advocates of a realistic approach to all types of euthanasia. He long ago rejected concepts like "purposeful suffering," contending that to embrace that notion is, logically, a rejection of *all* medical means intended to counteract pain.

As an example of a needlessly prolonged life, Fletcher cites the case of Jonathan Swift, the Irish satirist and clergyman, who over a period of several years gradually lost his mind. Swift's life, he contends, had lost its meaning when he lost his personality.

In his book *Morals and Medicine* (1954), Fletcher wrote, "It was a death degrading to [Swift] and to those close to him. His mind crumbled to pieces. It took him eight years to die while his brain rotted. He read the third chapter of Job on his birthday as long as he could see. 'And Job spake, and said, Let the day perish when I was born, and the night in which it was said, There is a man child conceived.' The pain in Swift's eye was so acute that it took five men to hold him down, to keep him from tearing out his eye with his own hands. For the last three years he sat and drooled. Knives had to be kept entirely out of his reach. When the end came, finally, his fits of convulsion lasted thirty-six hours."

Fletcher says of Swift's last years, "He was *demoralized*, without a vestige of true self-possession left in him. He wanted to commit what the law calls suicide and what vitalistic ethics calls sin. Standing by was some good doctor of physick, trembling with sympathy and frustration. Secretly, perhaps, he wanted to commit what the law calls murder. Both had full knowledge of the way out, which is half the foundation of moral integrity, but unlike his patient the physician felt he had no freedom to act, which is the other half of moral integrity. And so, meanwhile, necessity, blind and unmoral, irrational physiology and pathology, made the decision. It was in reality no decision at all, no moral behavior in the least, unless submission to physical ruin and spiritual disorganization can be called a decision and a moral choice. For let us not forget that in such tragic affairs there is a moral destruction, a spiritual disorder, as well as a physical degeneration. As Swift himself wrote to his niece fully five years before the end: 'I am so stupid and confounded that I

98

cannot express the mortification I am under both of body and soul.' "

According to Fletcher, for the man of moral integrity, the mere fact of being alive is not as important as the terms of that life, and when these terms are but a comatose state or a conscious condition just as helpless, then it is time to end it. Fletcher concluded that to shorten life is no more of an encroachment of God's power than to prolong life, and modern medicine does that constantly.

One of the Church of England's top theologians, Dr. Robert Mortimer, bishop of Exeter, has frequently proclaimed that/physicians need not use all medical techniques available to prolong the life of a dying person. He says that while there is a moral responsibility to maintain the life of old persons by ordinary means, there is no obligation to use "extraordinary" means, which he defines as medical procedures that "involve very great expenditure, inconvenience or hardship, and which at the same time offer no reasonable expectation of success or of benefit."

In a speech to a group of physicians, Bishop Mortimer explained that ordinary food and medicine should never be denied anyone, but "to subject the very old to the acute discomfort of a serious operation or of feeding by intravenous drip would seem to be morally wrong. Such means should be used only where there is reasonable hope of recovery or where some benefit of happiness is conferred on the patient."

A growing number of Protestant leaders are attacking the church for not assuming its full responsibility in the area of euthanasia. The church, they say, should be doing more to effect meaningful euthanasia legislation. They have also criticized the church for refusing to help relieve much of the life-and-death responsibility now resting solely upon doctors.

Reverend Leslie Weatherhead, a past president of the

Methodist Conference and the former minister of the City Temple in London, is one of the strongest advocates of this position. He calls himself an "enthusiastic" member of the Voluntary Euthanasia Society, and has many times said that it is unfair that all the responsibilities of euthanasia should be left to the merciful feelings of one doctor, or that a patient's release from pain should depend on one doctor's views.

"I sincerely believe," he wrote in *The Christian Agnostic* (1965), "that those who come after us will wonder why on earth we kept a human being alive against his own will, when all the dignity, beauty and meaning of life had vanished; when any gain to anyone was clearly impossible, and when we should have been punished by the State if we kept an animal alive in similar physical conditions. . . . I for one would be willing to give the patient the Holy Communion and stay with him while a doctor, whose responsibility I should share, allowed him to lay down his useless body and pass in dignity and peace into the next phase of being."

Jewish beliefs, too, generally coincide with those of the other religious groups in regard to passive euthanasia. At the Central Conference of American Rabbis in 1969, the following situation was posed for consideration: After a series of strokes, a patient lay near death. Two physicians—one of whom was the son of the ill man—agreed, with the consent of the rest of the family, to withhold all life-prolonging medication.

In evaluating this case, a committee at the Central Conference concluded: "If the patient is a hopelessly dying patient, the physician has no duty to keep him alive a little longer. He is entitled to die. If the physician attempts actively to hasten the death, that is against the ethics of Jewish law. In the case described, the physician is not really hastening the death; he has simply ceased his efforts to delay it."

100

Rabbi Immanuel Jacobovits, the authority on Jewish ethics, has written that Jewish laws allow the withholding of life-sustaining medication. In *Jewish Medical Ethics,* Jacobovits says that ". ., any form of active euthanasia is strictly prohibited and condemned as plain murder . . . anyone who kills a dying person is liable to the death penalty as a common murderer. At the same time, Jewish law sanctions the withdrawal of any factor—whether extraneous to the patient himself or not—which may artificially delay his demise in the final phase."

Jacobovits emphasizes, however, that the patient for whom such steps are considered must be expected to die within three days or less. Thus it may be impossible to justify passive euthanasia in the case of a patient who may yet live for weeks or months.

Are the major religions being realistic enough in their proclamations about euthanasia? Probably not. There seems to be little room for flexibility in their generally held firm stand against active euthanasia, and even their more liberal views concerning passive euthanasia rarely set down any definite guidelines as to when a patient is considered to be "dying" or "dead." In a time of phenomenal medical advances, the church has not risen to the challenge before it.

A twenty-eight-year-old engineer whose mother recently died has become a strong critic of organized religion. His mother was a devoutly religious person through most of her life, but as she lay dying from terminal cancer, her own condition caused her to question her own beliefs. Her son recalls how her pain and discomfort finally led her to pray for death—but her prayers went unanswered for a period of many weeks. The prayers eventually took on an angry tone, and soon she began to resent her entire religious background. In her last days of life, she cursed God for refusing to let her die.

101

A chaplain at a Southern California hospital told a UCLA conference on medicine and religion of the countless numbers of cases in which lives that are inhumanely prolonged pass the point of no return. He recalled one particular instance in which a patient was unconscious and nearly dead, but was kept functioning by around-the-clock hospital care, including intravenous feeding and a respirator. "She had no chance of survival, but the family wanted everything possible done," he said. "She was kept alive two weeks, then she died."

Chaplain Robert Reeves says, "We have in our society two supreme challenges. They are to find an honorable equivalent to Spartan exposure on the rocks at one end of life, and an honorable equivalent to the Eskimo hole in the ice at the other end of life. Other cultures have met these problems honorably. We have not."

Reeves believes that we have "perverted the Judeo-Christian tradition" into a doctrine that mere biological existence is of the utmost good, which has placed us in a dreadful ethical dilemma. He says that we should revert back to the thinking of our religious heritage, which placed the supreme value "on the personhood of man, the person in his wholeness, the person in his freedom, the person in his integrity and dignity. When illness brings a person to a state in which he is less than a free person, less than one with integrity and dignity, then what is most valuable and precious is gone, and we may well feel that his mere continuance by machine or drugs is a violation of him as a person."

Yet no matter what the religious objections to euthanasia may be, does the church have a right to dictate to the entire society as to what its legal statutes should be? Most jurists believe they do not. In fact, since secular affairs have always

102

been constitutionally separated from church affairs in the United States, religious influences upon all legal matters should always be considered irrelevant.

Referring to the First Amendment in a 1947 decision, the Supreme Court concluded, "Neither a state nor the federal government can set up a church. Neither can it pass laws which aid one religion, aid all religions, or prefer one religion to another."

In a later decision, Mr. Justice Frankfurter of the same court wrote, "If the primary end achieved by a form of regulation is the affirmation or promotion of religious doctrine—primarily, in the sense that all secular ends which it purportedly serves are derivative from, not wholly independent of, the advancement of religion—the regulation is beyond the power of the state."

As society continues to develop a new ethics, religious interests will undoubtedly carry less and less weight. There was once church opposition to such practices as relieving pain in childbirth and the use of anesthetics, but this resistance was eventually overcome. Despite continuing pressures from the Roman Catholic church, the abortion laws were recently liberalized. In turn, the religious opposition to euthanasia will also probably become less influential with the passage of time.

In discussing this subject, Glanville Williams wrote, "If it is true that euthanasia can be condemned only according to a religious opinion, this should be sufficient at the present day to remove the prohibition from the criminal law. The prohibition imposed by a religious belief should not be applied by law to those who do not share the belief, where this is not required for the worldly welfare of society generally."

According to Williams, ". . . the pretension of the moral theologian, sitting in the calm of his study, to dictatorial powers of moral interpretation must be rejected. The question, at least, is one for the patient himself, or else for the practical judgment of the medical practitioner, for these two alone know the hard and terrible facts of the last stages of malignant disease."

Thus, whether religious institutions oppose or support euthanasia, their opinions should be no more influential than those of anyone else. When legislatures consider changes in the euthanasia laws, they should be swayed by the secular arguments, not the religious ones.

Yet without some dramatic changes in our thinking, the tragic situation we find ourselves in of painfully prolonging lives in hopeless cases will continue. As Joseph Fletcher has written in *Harper's Magazine* (October 1960), "Unless we face up to the facts with moral sturdiness our hospitals and homes will become mausoleums where the inmates exist in a living death. In this day of 'existential' outlook, in its religious and nonreligious versions, we might think twice on Nietzsche's observation, 'In certain cases, it is indecent to go on living.' Perhaps it is a supreme lack of faith and self-respect to continue, as he put it, 'to vegetate in a state of cowardly dependence upon doctors and special treatments, once the meaning of life, the right to life, has been lost.' "

6. Death and Euthanasia: The Taboo Subjects

The topic of euthanasia has traditionally been avoided in public discussions because death itself is such a taboo subject in this society. Two million Americans die every year, yet as a people we go to great extremes to shun the reality of death, particularly our own.

Almost all other cultures have conceived of death as a natural process, even as the ultimate friend. But we hide from the thought of death, pretend it will not happen to us, and regard it as the ultimate enemy.

"People today view death as a sign of weakness, almost as something to be ashamed of," says one psychiatrist. "We demand that death be prevented at all cost, even when it is unavoidable. We make believe that we're going to live forever."

Thus, euthanasia is rarely seriously considered by most people. After all, they reason, death must always be challenged. Euthanasia would be giving in to an "evil." Ultimately, these people never face up to their own death until old age or a terminal disease forces them to. Until then, and sometimes even then, they are convinced that society will soon find a cure-all for whatever ails them. They view euthanasia as irrelevant.

Our Western culture also happens to be a youth-oriented one. The elderly are held in less esteem than their counterparts in many Eastern countries. Vigor, slimness, and a lack of wrinkles are admirable qualities here. In 1969, the buying public spent five billion dollars on cosmetics and other products designed to keep themselves looking younger. By comparison, in 1970 the federal government spent just 1.3 billion dollars on Old Age Assistance. No wonder the concepts of elderliness and dying are so taboo.

Dr. Florence Clothier, a former instructor in psychiatry at the Harvard Medical School, believes that death has now replaced sex as society's most forbidden topic of discussion. She sees parallels between the way we deal with death, and the way sex was once treated.

"Even for professional men and women," says Dr. Clothier, "euthanasia and death remain an almost taboo subject—just as sex was once taboo. Human sexuality, until Freud opened windows and doors, was not regarded as a fit subject for research or for education. Nevertheless, because of the nature of mankind, boys and girls and men and women were preoccupied with sex. It was not discussed directly, certainly not in mixed company. The tensions it created were mitigated in romantic daydreams, sentimental novels, in titillating wit, and in dirty jokes.

"During the twentieth century, it has been possible for

open discussion to replace suggestive innuendo on the subject of sex. Sexuality has been recognized as a suitable, even an essential, topic for study and research and for dialog between the generations and the sexes."

In much the same way, Dr. Clothier believes that we are now approaching death unrealistically, making subjects like euthanasia taboo. "Death remains a reality which relatively few can accept or face," she says. "Man tries to live as if it could not happen to him or to those he loves. At the same time, he lives under a primitive shadow of fear. When death of a patient, child or loved one occurs, he suffers not only grief but also a sense of guilt for 'not having done more' or for past expressions of hostility or even hostile thoughts."

The obstacles which the Euthanasia Educational Fund faces in its educational programs are overwhelming. How, in fact, do you convince people to confront their own dying and death when many of our major institutions—from health agencies to hospitals to religious groups—encourage us to deal so unrealistically with death.

Hospitals, for example, are laboratories of eternal optimism. Technological advances have convinced us that a solution can be found for all our ills—including death. Terminal patients are often not told the gravity of their illnesses, and are misled to believe that recovery—not death—is just around the corner.

Many of the major religions teach us that death is really not death at all. Man is immortal, they say, and death is merely a passage from one state of existence to another. One can have a pleasant eternal life if he simply adheres to this set of religious beliefs or that one.

There are even alternatives in our society for those who reject all religious dogmas but who still cannot accept the reality of death. Cryonics, for example, promises to freeze your body for an indefinite number of years or centuries until cures are found for all diseases, and means are developed to prevent natural death. In 1967, a retired psychology professor in Glendale, California, was dying of lung cancer. Before he died, however, he paid a $4,000 fee in order to become the first man ever to have his body indefinitely frozen by the cryonics method.

Organizations like the Cryonics Society, the Life Extension Society, and the Society for Biosis are now operating in many sections of the country. They tell man that he can be made immortal here on earth. One of the newsletters of the Life Extension Society includes a poem entitled "My Will: To Be an Icecube."

Certainly one of the greatest perpetuators of an unrealistic conception of death is the funeral industry. "It is phenomenal the extent that undertakers go to in order to deny that death ever occurs," says one psychiatrist. "They use cosmetics to beautify the corpse, hoping that it won't look dead at all. They instill in you the fantasy that the dead person is sleeping peacefully, creating a false illusion of life. They employ euphemisms that disguise and repress the presence of death—phrases like 'passed away' and 'resting quietly in the slumber room.' "

How can we relate to death realistically when funeral homes sell coffins equipped with innerspring mattresses and "the revolutionary 'Perfect-Posture' bed"? Or when the deceased is dressed in "handmade original fashions—styles from the best in life for the last memory"?

No wonder we can't deal with death when we are finally forced to confront it. California sociologist Robert Fulton estimates that the average American family often goes twenty years without encountering death. Children growing up in the television era are so shielded from the realities of natural death that when informed that their grandfather has died, they respond with the question, "Who shot him?"

"When we ask the public—particularly those who are young or middle-aged—to think now about the circumstances of their dying, we are often met by puzzled looks," says Elizabeth T. Halsey of the Euthanasia Educational Fund. "Many people have just not accepted death as inevitable. And euthanasia can't be considered seriously if the subject of death itself is so consciously avoided."

The way the public shies away from death was revealed in an experiment conducted by Wayne State's Center for Psychological Studies of Dying, Death and Lethal Behavior. The participants in the study were a group of housewives whose stated attitudes toward death ranged from an intense fear to a calm acceptance. The women were brought to the hospital ward and were instructed to visit with patients, some of whom, they were told, were terminal cases. No matter what they said their own views on death were, all the women avoided the dying patients as much as possible, cutting conversations short and avoiding eye-to-eye contact with them. But with those patients who they were told were recovering, the women freely conversed.

This death taboo was brought home to Lael Wertenbaker, the former *Time* correspondent, when she was scheduled to speak at the University of North Carolina on the "right to die." She had written the book *Death of a Man* (1957) about her husband's death via voluntary euthanasia.

In the book, Mrs. Wertenbaker describes how her husband resisted his doctor's advice and refused prolonged hospital care. He carried on the last stages of his life as normally as possible, and finally decided to relieve himself from his terminal disease by ending his life. In her book, Mrs. Werten-baker emphasizes how her husband lived his days the way he wished, and not as some hospital staff wanted him to.

Before Mrs. Wertenbaker appeared for her lecture on the North Carolina campus, some members of the faculty ob-jected to her speaking on the subject of a man who tech-nically committed suicide.

"It was suicide technically," she recalled recently at a meeting of the Euthanasia Conference in New York City. "But on the other hand it was no rejection of life, which he loved. It was a 'choosing of the moment,' it was the cup of hemlock when you are already under sentence of death. It was not suicide in rejection to being alive at all.

"However, [the faculty] thought that this was a depressing subject and that some tender little adolescent would go out into the night and shoot himself. So the professors said with great regret, 'We consider this too dangerous a subject, more dangerous than sex to talk about.' And I said, 'Well, if anybody committed suicide after my talk I'd be very much surprised, because Wertenbaker's death was an affirmation of life, which was the reason for writing about it.'

"So they agreed to let me give this lecture. I said to the students, 'You are being treated as grown-up people. Death is a fact and therefore let us talk about it, and let us talk about the right to die and the fact that life should come to an end properly.'

"The students were marvelous, and the next day, two of them came up and said, 'Oh, Mrs. Wertenbaker, being at that lecture yesterday made us glad to be alive.'"

Mrs. Wertenbaker looks back with no regrets at the way her husband chose to die. She says that he "had his deathbed, his last moments with each of us in the knowledge that they were last moments, and this is quite tremendous. This was his way to go out, and a very proper way.

"At the time when he decided, of his own right as a grown-up man, that the time had come—that the rest of the time he had left to live would be either doped up or in pain or would have meant lack of efficient control of function— this was the point at which he could die literally on his own feet. This is the way he wished to go."

As mentioned in a previous chapter, even doctors and nurses sometimes have trouble facing death realistically. Some years ago, a research project compared the amount of time it took nurses to respond to calls from terminal patients as opposed to the time needed to answer calls from non-terminal cases. The study found that there was a much greater delay in responding to the dying patients.

Dr. Elisabeth Kubler-Ross, whose interviews with the dying have been the most comprehensive ever conducted, relates the following incident in her book *On Death and Dying* (1969): "Early in my work with dying patients I observed the desperate need of the hospital staff to deny the existence of terminally ill patients on their ward. In another hospital I once spent hours looking for a patient capable to be interviewed, only to be told that there was no one fatally ill and able to talk. On my walk through the ward I saw an old man reading a paper with the headline 'Old soldiers never die.' He looked seriously ill and I asked him if it did not scare him to 'read about that.' He looked at me with anger and disgust, telling me that I must be one of those physicians who can only care for a patient as long as he is well but when it comes to dying, then we all shy away from them."

There is little doubt that death and euthanasia are so difficult to confront partly because we have made dying such

111

an impersonal and lonely process. In earlier times, a dying person knew that death was near, and he was able to prepare for it. He usually died at home in familiar surroundings and near those whom he loved. He was able to have final words with each one of them.

But this traditional deathbed scene is now a thing of the past. Today, 75 percent of all deaths occur in crowded institutions (like hospitals and nursing homes). Modern man dies without the security of familiar places or faces. He is often sedated and betubed, and is rarely consulted about the treatment he is to receive. If he is in "intensive care," he will be shielded from his family much of the time.

Dr. Kubler-Ross describes the typical frightening hospital experience. "Dying becomes lonely and impersonal because the patient is often taken out of his familiar environment and rushed to an emergency room. Whoever has been very sick and has required rest and comfort especially may recall his experience of being put on a stretcher and enduring the noise of the ambulance siren and hectic rush until the hospital gates open. Only those who have lived through this may appreciate the discomfort and cold necessity of such transportation which is only the beginning of a long ordeal—hard to endure when you are well, difficult to express in words when noise, light, pumps, and voices are all too much to put up with. It may well be that we might consider more the patient under the sheets and blankets and perhaps stop our well-meant efficiency and rush, in order to hold the patient's hand, to smile, or to listen to a question. I include the trip to the hospital as the first episode in dying, as it is for many."

The added stress of the hospital environment takes its toll not only on the patient, but on his family, too. One study has found that within a year following the death of a family member, the death rate among relatives is twice as high if the primary death has occurred in a hospital as opposed to the home.

Marjorie A. Beckman, assistant director of social services at Lenox Hill Hospital in New York, says, "Any visitor to an intensive care unit in a medical institution would be appalled—typewriters go, bells ring, lights light, and the whole milieu is one of crisis and very little human contact. At the time when the patient is most critically ill, the support and visits of his family, friends or relatives is severely curtailed and the closest thing to him is a monitoring machine."

Consider the recent case of a teenage girl dying of leukemia in a public hospital. Her last hours were spent under the bright lights of an intensive care room, with tubes and machines surrounding her. Her parents were relegated to a room down the hall, where they were forced to wait for the five minutes of visiting time they were allowed with her each hour.

Reverend Carl Nighswonger, a chaplain in a Chicago hospital, thinks that such a situation is unjustifiable. "In twelve years of hospital chaplaincy," he says, "I have yet to find a family that could cycle their grief according to the hospital schedule. How much better it would be, when the doctors give up, if the patient could be moved to a dimly lit, quiet room where the family could sit at his bedside and hold his hand."

In an article in the *Journal of the American Medical Association* (September 29, 1962), Dr. Frank J. Ayd describes the reactions of the family in such a situation. "They resent being deprived of the opportunity to share the waning moments of life with the one they love," writes Dr. Ayd. "For years they have shared joys and heartaches. Why, when they could face the greatest of all crises together, must they be shoved out of the room, displaced by gadgets and personnel striving to delay the inevitable?"

Proponents of voluntary euthanasia maintain that the terminally ill patient should be allowed to decide for himself whether extraordinary measures prolonging his life should be continued. But standard procedures among many doctors make it impossible for a patient to make such a decision, since patients with incurable diseases are often never informed of the true nature of their illnesses. In too many cases, they are not told that death is inevitable and that life-sustaining treatment is futile.

The *Medical World News* has cited studies which show that from 69 to 90 percent of the physician population are opposed to telling the patient that his illness is terminal. Doctors and relatives, in an attempt to protect the feelings of the dying person, frequently use all types of devious means to avoid revealing the truth to him.

One doctor admits that in medical school, "I was taught to lie to my patients. This deception was supposed to begin when you tell a youngster, 'This polio shot won't hurt a bit,' and it continues right through the final lies that come in the last stages of life."

Doctors will offer false hopes even when death is obvious and frequently employ enough medical jargon to leave the sick person totally confused.

Is this deception justifiable, even under the pretense of protecting the patient from unwelcome news? "To deny a person accurate knowledge about something as crucial as his own health is disgusting," says one hospital chaplain. "Yet it's done countless numbers of times in every hospital in the country. A patient deserves to be told that he is about to die, if he is. Dying is part of the life process, and to deprive a person of a full understanding of his fate is to deny him an insight into life that is rightfully his."

When patients are honestly informed of the true nature of

their terminal illness, it affords them the opportunity to take care of matters they otherwise might not have. They can put their financial affairs in order, articulate important feelings to family members and friends, and make peace with God. They can also experience the feeling of being in control of the decisions which must be made in their last remaining weeks.

Renée Rox, in her book *Experiment Perilous* (1959), wrote about a hospital in which all terminal patients were told about their fatal diseases. The open communication among patients and staff helped ease the apprehensions of dying and death for all concerned. Patients were able to help and comfort each other, and could realistically attend to dozens of matters, from letter writing to planning for the futures of their family members.

Robert Kavanaugh, an instructor of thanatology at the University of California at San Diego, believes that there are very few instances in which the truth should be withheld from a patient. Kavanaugh, who has written a book called *Facing Death* (1972), says, "Any doctor who doesn't tell a rational and nonsenile patient his true condition is being very unethical. That's a basic right that just can't be justifiably denied to anyone, even children. My own experience with children is that we greatly underestimate them. At times, they may not appear as mature as they really are, because they'll play any games their parents want them to so as not to be rejected. But they see enough death-bed scenes on television to know what's happening."

Two researchers at the National Cancer Institute also found children to be more mature than is normally assumed. They interviewed fifty-one youngsters being treated for leukemia at the institute in Bethesda, Maryland. Their conclusion was that children should never be sheltered from the truth. They found that when tactfully informed of their

115

illness, youngsters could accept it without any serious traumatic effects.

At institutions like Children's Hospital in Los Angeles, each case involving a terminally ill child is dealt with on an individual basis. If the parents feel the youngster is emotionally capable of accepting the truth about his illness, then he is told honestly about his disease. But many parents want the truth concealed from their child, and the staff cooperates with them.

The most frequent complaint of seriously ill patients is that rarely will someone sit down with them and discuss their illness. Yet according to a study in a Southern California hospital, 82 percent of the patients interviewed wanted to be told an accurate diagnosis of their disease, no matter how severe it was. However, hospitals often treat the patient as the last person to be consulted when decisions are made about the treatment. At a time when the patient desperately longs for someone to talk honestly with him, the wall of estrangement between him and those around him intensifies.

In her book, *On Death and Dying*, Dr. Kubler-Ross describes the typical hospital situation. "When a patient is severely ill, he is often treated like a person with no right to an opinion. It is often someone else who makes the decision if and when and where a patient should be hospitalized. It could take so little to remember that the sick person too has feelings, has wishes and opinions, and has—most important of all—the right to be heard . . .

"He may cry for rest, peace and dignity, but he will get infusions, transfusions, a heart machine, or tracheotomy if necessary. He may want one single person to stop for one single minute so he can ask one single question—but he will get a dozen people around the clock, all busily preoccupied with his heart rate, pulse, electrocardiogram or pulmonary functions, his secretions or excretions but not with him as a human being. He may wish to fight it all but it is going to be a useless fight since all this is done in the fight for his life, and if they can save his life they can consider the person afterwards. Those who consider the person first may lose precious time to save his life! At least this seems to be the rationale or justification behind all this—or is it? Is the reason for this increasingly mechanical, depersonalized approach our own defensiveness? Is this approach our own way to cope with and repress the anxieties that a terminally or critically ill patient evokes in us? Is our concentration on equipment, on blood pressure, our desperate attempt to deny the impending death which is so frightening and discomforting to us that we displace all our knowledge onto machines, since they are less close to us than the suffering face of another human being which would remind us once more of our lack of omnipotence, our own limits and failures, and last but not least perhaps our own mortality?

"Maybe the question has to be raised: Are we becoming less human or more human?"

In spite of attempts to withhold the truth, most people who are dying know it anyway. Cancer specialists say that their patients often realize the nature of their disease even if they're never told. Studies seem to support this contention.

Dr. J. M. Hinton, a London psychiatrist, conducted an extensive investigation into the behavior and thoughts of fatally ill patients at Kings College Hospital. The dying patients were interviewed regularly. At the same time, control patients in the same rooms under the care of the same doctors were also interviewed. These controls provided a basis of comparison, and also helped relieve any feelings the dying patients may have had that they were being singled out for the interviews because of their specific illness. Dr. Hinton found that distress was significantly more common in the dying patients, and as many as 75 percent said they believed their disease was fatal.

Similar findings have been observed by Dr. Kubler-Ross. She discovered that the fatally ill patient inevitably finds out the truth, and is then often resentful that the information has been withheld from him, even if with good intentions. The biggest fear of the dying patient, she says, is not death itself, but the painful circumstances of false cheerfulness, lies, and isolation that he is put through.

Patients often find out about their illness in unconventional ways. They may sneak a peek at their medical records. One woman discovered the seriousness of her condition when she casually ran across an article in *Newsweek* which described her illness down to the last symptom.

The sick person frequently picks up cues from those around him, particularly the way doctors and nurses act when they are nearby. Relatives and friends also provide revealing cues with their smiling faces which can never quite conceal the grief and tension they actually feel.

Yet even after the patient discovers the true nature of his illness, the conspiracy of silence often continues. A middle-aged man was in a hospital recently, suffering from terminal cancer of the pancreas. The hospital staff assumed that he was unaware of his condition, and the resident surgeon told him his illness was due to gall bladder problems, and he would eventually get better. However, the patient had actually surmised the malignancy on his own. But because everyone was deceiving him, he felt alienated and insecure about discussing the disease with doctors. After many days of mental anguish, he finally burst into tears while talking with a psychiatrist in a patient-care conference. He related how he had guessed all along about the cancer, and pleaded for someone to discuss his illness realistically with him.

Dr. Stanford B. Friedman of the department of pediatrics and psychiatry at the University of Rochester related a similar story at a 1971 two-day conference on "The Patient, Death and the Family." Said Dr. Friedman, "Sixteen-year-old Fred was dying of leukemia. His doctor wanted to discuss his illness with him but Fred's parents refused and circumvented the boy's questions. Finally Fred asked the same questions of his doctors and nurses, then confronted them all with the discrepancies in their replies. He told his parents that he no longer believed them, that he knew he was going to die and how he wanted his favorite belongings disposed of."

Unlike most patients, Fred spoke up and demanded to know the truth.

Those doctors that are informing their patients of the severity of their illnesses are finding some remarkable results. Many patients express relief that they are finally allowed to share some of their own fears and anxieties with someone else. Others—including children—are actually participating in decisions involving the possibility of their own euthanasia.

Robert Kavanaugh of the University of California at San Diego recalls a case he was involved in recently. A ten-year-old boy was dying of cancer. "The illness had dragged on for three years, and had left the family bankrupt," says Kavanaugh. "The boy's doctor came to me one day, very frustrated, saying that he had a new drug that could keep the boy alive in a lingering existence for two more years. He wondered whether the administering of the drug would be worthwhile, since the quality of the boy's life would be less than ideal.

"I brought the parents, the doctor and the boy together so

119

they could talk it over," continues Kavanaugh. "It was the first time the boy had discussed his illness with anyone. Up to that point, his parents had put up a pretense of cheerfulness and had never told the boy about the severe nature of his illness.

"Everyone had their say about whether the drug should be administered. It was a joint decision when they all finally agreed to give the boy the drug for six months, at which time they would meet again to discuss if they were going to extend it for another six months."

Cases like this one are rare. Even in instances where the patient is informed that he is terminally ill, he is given little or no voice in determining the extent of his own treatment. A forty-one-year-old woman, whose seventy-year-old mother recently died, now regrets not listening to the pleas of her mother for a quick end to her prolonged illness. "The last weeks of her life were long and agonizing," she says. "So many times when I would visit her, she'd ask me, 'Why don't you help me die?' Looking back, I wonder why we didn't. It was wrong to let her needlessly suffer like she did. She was ready to die a month before the doctors finally let her go."

The family's subsequent guilt feelings are sometimes even worse when the patient is not told the truth about his illness. Playwright Robert Anderson has admitted to the grief he still feels because of not informing his wife that she had cancer, even though he knew it four years before she died. Anderson, author of *I Never Sang for My Father* and *Tea and Sympathy,* articulated his feelings at a 1971 conference on death sponsored by the Rochester (N.Y.) General Hospital. "It would have been easier, far, far less lonely, if she had known," he admitted. "I would want to know. The complicated ruses, deceptions, explanations, were incredible.

"I'm quite sure I deprived my wife of the right to share her dying with someone else. I played God for four years, trying to arrange her life in a way I thought she would want to lead it in her last years, but actually might not have led it if she had known they were her last years."

7. The Rights of the Dying Patient

Sometimes it seems that the only people who can face up to death are the dying. When euthanasia is discussed, often it is the elderly and the dying who have the least anxieties about examining it realistically.

Dolores is sixty-six years old. In April 1972, her doctors told her she had no more than a year to live—a victim of cancer. When you read this, she will probably already have died.

"The tragedy of dying is not only death itself, and the helplessness you feel at the hands of death," she said in an interview four weeks after finding out about her fatal disease. "But there's another kind of helplessness, too. It's the knowledge that once the time for death arrives, those around me will postpone it long after it's practical to do so.

"I've been in hospitals before, in some very uncomfortable situations," she said. "And I've always been willing to withstand the discomfort and pain, because I knew I would eventually recover and get back on my feet.

"But this time, going to that hospital worries me. If I have to die, I don't know why I must spend my last few days or weeks in as pitiful circumstances as possible. Why will they have to stick needles in me just to prolong the agony for a little while longer? It doesn't make sense.

"I just want to be allowed to die comfortably and painlessly. And if that means bringing the end about a little sooner than it might have otherwise happened, I have no objections to that. If that's what you call euthanasia, then I'm in favor of it. As the days go on and the pain gets worse, I think I'm going to be talking about euthanasia with those around me more and more."

Should people like Dolores have the legal right to decide whether euthanasia should be administered? At a 1972 conference in San Francisco on the ethics of life and death, it was often suggested that terminally ill patients should play a bigger role in deciding their own fate.

The conference was cosponsored by the American Association of University Women and the Institute of Society, Ethics and the Life Sciences. Recommendations were made that a patient deserves the right to know he is dying if he wants such information; that he should have the right to appraise his own condition—with complete access to his medical chart—and help determine further treatment; and that he should be able to refuse any treatment that may preclude a dignified and peaceful death.

Perhaps Robert, a twenty-one-year old student, might have chosen to die with dignity if he had been given the chance. He had leukemia, was told about the disease, and realized the odds were against him. After more than a year of living with the illness he was admitted to a hospital on New Year's Eve, in critical condition, near death. He was taken to the intensive care room, and the hospital staff kept his parents informed of his condition as they sat in the waiting room.

Dr. Elisabeth Kubler-Ross, an authority on death and dying, visited the patient in the hospital. And in an October 1971 article in *The Canadian Nurse,* she related what the ensuing ordeal was like.

"There before me," she wrote, "lay this handsome young man, Robert—blown up, tubes hanging out of his mouth, lips cut, infusion bottles running, the tracheotomy, the respirator—the whole works. But what first bothered me was that he was naked from head to toe! Why? I took a bedsheet to cover him up, only to be told, 'Don't bother, he's going to push it off again, anyway.' Angered by this I said, 'Give me two safety pins.'

"When I walked over to him, he took my hand and looked up to the ceiling. My first thought was that he was telling me he was ready to die. But then I noticed a strong light shining in his eyes. When I asked if these lights could be dimmed or switched off, I was instead lectured about the rules and regulations of the intensive care unit. Naturally, I became more angry and more disappointed."

Dr. Kubler-Ross also asked for two chairs so that Robert's parents could sit near his side rather than out in the waiting room. But she was told that the parents could not have a chair because during the previous hour they had visited more than the permissible five minutes.

A few hours later, Robert died—with tubes in his mouth, with the respirator going, with the bright lights still glaring in his eyes—and with his parents sitting outside in the waiting room.

Dr. Kubler-Ross does not criticize the medical care that Robert received. But she feels the doctors did not fulfill their complete responsibility to either the patient or his parents. She said that the physicians "acknowledged at 7:00 P.M. New Year's Eve that he was dying, they conveyed the message beautifully and tactfully to the parents, and then they left. If they had really felt deep down inside that they had been marvelous, wonderful physicians, that they had done everything good physicians could do, that it was all right to die, they would have taken Robert out of the intensive care unit at 7:00 P.M. and put him in a small room—a private room with a dim light, and two chairs for his parents to sit in. And he would have died in the presence of his parents, in peace and dignity."

Cases like this occur constantly in hospitals. Patients who are dying are subjected to treatment that sometimes seems less than human. And occasionally, they are turned into nothing more than guinea pigs for tests that mean nothing to them.

In a New York hospital early in 1972, a patient lay in a coma, and doctors had given up all hope for his recovery. But one physician ordered the nurses to give the patient a blood-flow test in conjunction with a national research study on cerebral death. This test, which measured oxygenation in the brain, entailed threading tubes through the blood vessels of the neck and up into the brain. One of the nurses on the ward said she was in favor of the national study, "but not if it interferes with a patient's dignity in dying." Said the nurse, "Cramming an endotracheal tube down a seventy-eight-year-old man's throat, or banging away and shocking him to make his heart start so he can 'live' for another twenty-four hours in abject misery, is wrong. And it degrades us as well as the patient and his family."

In another experiment in New York, two physicians injected live cancer cells into twenty-two patients at the Jewish Chronic Disease Hospital. The purpose of the test was to evaluate the immune-response mechanism in the seriously ill. But contrary to all medical ethics, the doctors disregarded their responsibility to notify the patients of the type of cell that was to be injected. The physicians were later accused of fraudulently obtaining the consent of the patients, and their licenses were suspended for one year.

The treatment that the elderly and the ill receive in many nursing homes is often just as contemptible. The subhuman care in some nursing homes has been documented in many studies. The Better Government Association conducted a sweeping investigation of nursing homes in the Chicago area in 1971, and uncovered conditions that were "shocking, almost beyond belief." Its report said that patients in some of these institutions often live without decency or human dignity.

BGA investigators found elderly sick people who had to sleep at night in terribly cold rooms with only ragged blankets to cover them. There were often not enough blankets for everyone, so patients frequently fought over them.

The number of instances of personal indignities in nursing homes was endless. A BGA representative witnessed two attendants who were helping an ill ninety-year-old man into a tub for his weekly bath. The elderly patient asked, "Please don't push me so fast, my legs don't bend as fast as they used to." One of the attendants then struck him in the face, and the old man let out a scream as he fell into the tub.

A woman patient was grabbed like an animal and fed a meat patty that was slapped into her mouth. The woman choked on the food and was dragged to bed for her "misbehavior."

Many of those in nursing homes were found to be so close to death that they should have been under the constant supervision of a doctor. But they were kept in the nursing facilities because their presence guaranteed that state moneys would continue to flow into the homes.

As one elderly patient said, "We are the living dead. Look around at these people. We're all worn out and we just keep on living. We'd be better off dead."

Another investigation, this one nationwide, was made in 1970 by Ralph Nadar and six assistants. The Nadar study group uncovered miserable conditions similar to those described in the Chicago report. It found that drug companies often administered experimental drugs to residents of nursing homes without the consent of either the recipient or his family. Patients were abused almost as a daily part of their existence. Not only were their physical needs neglected, but they were mentally and emotionally abused, too. Nursing home patients were treated like children, chided when they wet their beds, and made to feel more helpless than they really were.

Congressman David Pryor of Arkansas, who studied nursing home care for sixteen months, has said, "We have turned over the sickest, the most helpless and the most vulnerable patient group in the medical care system to the most loosely controlled and least responsible faction of that system."

Pryor, who worked anonymously as a volunteer nurse's aide at several nursing homes, says, "I saw older citizens placed in homes which in some instances were excellent, bright, cheerful and well managed. But there were others which could have been created within the pages of a Charles Dickens novel. I saw loneliness and despair. I saw filth and anxiety."

Nursing homes, says Pryor, are big business and the stock

of many nursing home chains is highly sought by the exchanges. "We are commercializing our aged. Our citizens in nursing homes today have become in some instances mere human Ping-Pong balls on Wall Street."

No wonder one nurse wrote to Congressman Pryor: "I'm sick of the silent eyes of old people who have no one left; forced to die in a place that has no regard for their dignity or worth as human beings. . . . If we have the means to keep them alive, we have the means to allow them to live a meaningful old age."

Perhaps an advertisement for the *Medical World News* that appeared in the July 13, 1970, issue of *Advertising Age* summed it up best: "The Eskimos used to freeze their old people to death; we bury ours alive. Maybe the Eskimos were more merciful than we are. Ask the old people in nursing homes across the country. A fast death is a blessing we deny them. Yet we deny them a human life, too. For these people life is an endless succession of deprivations. The food is poor and there's not enough of it. A typical dinner at one Medicare-approved home consisted of one chicken wing and a scoop of dried-up potatoes. Insanitary conditions, lack of medical care, uncaring, sometimes deliberately cruel attendants, lack of even the barest safety precautions against fire or accident, are all facts of life for these patients. Perhaps worst of all, there is nothing to do—day in and day out—but wait for death to come."

Is this the kind of treatment we want for our ill and elderly? Is it any wonder that so many of the dying want the legal alternative of the "blessing" of "a fast death"?

An Arkansas woman cannot understand some of the obvious contradictions that prevent people from painlessly escaping from a prolonged and terminal illness. Her father and mother, both in their nineties, are in nursing homes, need maximum care, and "would very much like to say good-bye to this world." She tells of watching them suffer through broken hips, Parkinson's disease, kidney infections—and now cancer.

"It seems odd," she explains, "that people can legally make wills, dispose of property and such—but we do not have the right to say anything if we decide that the time has come for us to leave this world. Everyone accepts the fact that it is humane and just to have our animal friends put away rather than have us or them suffer."

Supporters of the liberalization of euthanasia laws believe that, if given the opportunity, many patients dying of terminal diseases would choose euthanasia over a prolonged and painful death. They point to the statistics that up to 500,000 cancer deaths occur in the United States each year. At least a percentage of these people, they reason, would choose euthanasia, and thus should be allowed to have that free choice.

But even without changes in the laws, euthanasia is sometimes being practiced discreetly—with the life-and-death decisions being made by doctors, patients, or relatives. Take the case of Ray, a middle-aged man dying of cancer of the brain. The cobalt treatments he was undergoing were helping him, but they had many side effects. Ray's hair was falling out, and he suffered vomiting attacks and fainting spells after the treatments. His pain increased with time, he became blind, began losing his memory, and lost eighty pounds. Finally his wife ordered his doctor to do nothing more except keep her husband as comfortable and pain-free as possible. He died a short time later.

"I guess," said Ray's wife, "you could call it a sort of euthanasia—a mercy killing—but when I get too bad, I hope somebody will love me enough, the way I loved Ray, and do the same for me."

At another hospital, the doctors and family agreed to let a three-year-old boy with leukemia die without extraordinary lifesaving methods being taken—but only after much indecision. The child, whose name was Robbie, was brought into the hospital in the final stages of his illness. The boy soon went into a coma, and breathing became so difficult that an oxygen tent was brought in. Doctors agreed that the degenerative process was irreversible, but still lifesaving procedures continued. Drugs were administered; a pillow was placed beneath the child's back, and his head was tilted back; a tracheotomy tube was inserted down his throat. Robbie began bleeding from the nose. Doctors knew that if he survived this ordeal he would have to go through it again— and soon. But still, they continued their efforts.

Finally, Robbie's father could take it no longer. He began asking whether these measures were really necessary. After much discussion, the doctors agreed to withdraw most of the life-prolonging procedures. Robbie was made to look comfortable, and his parents were readmitted to the room. He died as they held his hand.

A mother recently questioned why her son was not allowed to die after a motorcycle accident. At a meeting of the Voluntary Euthanasia Society in London, she told of the accident her eighteen-year-old son had been in two years earlier. She said that the boy had in fact "died" in the crash. "But he was resuscitated for eight minutes," she continued, "and as a result my son is doomed to a life of hospitalization and is paralyzed. He suffered deep brain injury.

"We have tried to help my son out of his misery, but where can an ordinary working-class person find a doctor who could do this with compassion for my son?"

As a patient at a Los Angeles nursing home said, "People are not allowed to die peacefully anymore. So many of my friends have been killed by cancer, and it's so terrible to see them so weak and full of pain. No matter what anyone tells you, drugs can't stop all the suffering. People shouldn't have to go through all of that. There should be an easier way out."

Some terminally ill patients are finding a quick means of escape. When doctors refuse to consider a patient's request for voluntary euthanasia, the desperate sufferer will sometimes do whatever he must to release himself from his agony. Studies reveal that as many as 18 percent of all suicides are committed by people suffering from severe illnesses, usually cancer. There are instances of patients swallowing Kleenex to suffocate themselves, and others who pull out tubes from their veins and noses, stopping the flow of life-sustaining medication. Technically, they have committed suicide; in human terms, they have freed themselves from circumstances they felt were intolerable.

Relatives who have watched their loved ones die dehumanizing deaths have frequently vowed not to let the same thing happen to them. A Missouri woman recalls how her mother-in-law died slowly over a period of four months. "She wished for death, knowing that her condition could only get worse," the woman says. "To be in constant pain and to have reached the point where none of the bodily functions are in working order is too much for an old person who has lived a proud, productive and useful life. It was painful for my husband and me to watch her slowly die before our very eyes, and when the end mercifully came, we were happy that she was finally at rest.

"Of one thing I am determined—my own life must not end in this manner. Somehow I must contrive to terminate it before I ever reach this stage."

As long ago as 1931, the British Reverend Peter Green argued that to force a person into such a suicidal situation alienates him from everything he has loved during his life. In

The Problem of Right Conduct, Reverend Green, the canon of Manchester, wrote, "Many men every year do commit suicide to escape lingering agony. But they do it in a spirit of angry revolt against God; they die without the consolation of religion; they lose the whole of any insurance they have made for wife and children; they shock their loved ones, and outrage public opinion. In such a case I should myself like my doctor, in conjunction with a specialist, to be allowed to state that the disease was fatal and likely to be slow and painful; and then I might be permitted to end my life at once in some painless manner."

In Illinois, a husband whose wife had been hopelessly crippled with arthritis for many years found that the legal alternatives available to them were not enough. As a last resort, he suffocated her at her own request. The man pleaded guilty to a manslaughter charge and was convicted. However, testimony was heard from the defendant's children and minister on what a devoted husband he had been, and the victim's doctor described the endless pain that she had endured.

After evaluating these statements, the judge—in an extraordinary move—allowed the defendant to withdraw his plea and enter a new plea of not guilty. The judge then dropped all charges, and allowed the man ". . . to go home . . . and live out the rest of [his] life in as much peace as [he] can find it in [his] heart to have."

The complex circumstances of modern medicine have led some doctors to compassionate acts that they may have once never considered doing. Consider the case of a close female relative of a physician who was dying of cancer. The doctor decided that any further life-prolonging hospital treatment was useless and inhumane, and the family brought their loved one home. Her body fluids were not replaced intravenously, nor was she forced to eat when it was painful to do so. No

133

antibiotics, oxygen, or blood were given to her. She took only pain-killing drugs to keep her reasonably comfortable and allow her to rest. "She died with dignity and in peace," says the doctor, "with only her family around her to show her their love. I have never regretted that we chose to let her die this way."

Dr. Edward H. Rynearson of the Mayo Clinic admits to carrying out passive euthanasia many times. "It is wrong for doctors to see how long we can keep 'vegetables' going," he says. "I want no part of it for my family, myself or my patients."

In one case, Dr. Rynearson says, he jerked out the intravenous tubes from a patient with hopeless cancer. Afterwards, he went to the administrative sister of the hospital, a Roman Catholic institution, and informed her of what he had just done. "She asked, bless her, if there was any way 'I can have you as a doctor when my time comes.' "

Dr. Rynearson believes that in most cases, the doctor should make the decision of when euthanasia should be administered. "I'm not talking about cases that are in doubt," he says, "but of patients who have had two or three operations, radiation and all the rest and who are still lying there screaming in pain. With enough tubes in a person and surrounded by oxygen, there is hardly any way he can die."

Dr. Pierre H. Muller, a well-known French physician, agrees that there comes a time when prolonging a life artificially becomes a vain action. In a September-October 1967 article in the *World Medical Journal,* Dr. Muller wrote, "Once he is certain that the nervous system is dead and no longer able to take over its controlling functions in the body, the doctor should give up the struggle on his own responsibility. Clearly he cannot ask the opinions of the family or their permission to stop maintenance of vegetative life, but he must collect all the relevant clinical, biological, and electro-encephalographic information and maybe after consultation with others participating in the maintenance work draw up a statement justifying his decision to abandon his efforts. If his action is challenged by any authority, he will then have the means to defend his decision."

Some medical schools are now beginning to confront death more realistically. A few of them have recently added instruction on death to their curriculum. And as more medical students learn to better deal with the circumstances of death, many of them are beginning to reject the long-accepted medical practice of sustaining life under all conditions. *The National Observer* (March 4, 1972) reported on a survey taken at the University of Washington, in which 90 percent of the fourth-year medical students supported passive euthanasia. Slightly less than half, 46 percent, favored active euthanasia, too.

Medical schools may even be able to do more to prepare their students for a realistic approach to death. Some doctors have recommended that programs of premortem care be established. Under such a plan, students in medical schools would receive specific practical training in caring for the dying. They would be taught to see themselves not as invincible conquerors of disease, but as human beings who sometimes can do nothing more for a patient than make his dying as comfortable as possible.

It has also been recommended that universities institute "life conferences" to parallel their "death conferences." In many medical schools, these "death conferences" are held after a patient dies so students can clinically discuss the treatments that were given to the deceased. An obvious counterpart would be "life conferences" to be held before the patient dies, in order to discuss what can be done to assist the patient and his family through their crisis, and help ease the grief, depression, and fears they may be experiencing.

But even with these changes, the burden of responsibility for administering euthanasia would still rest solely on the doctor. And although physicians like Dr. Rynearson maintain that no one is in a better position to assume that responsibility, many others feel that the burden should be shared. Robert Kavanaugh of the University of California at San Diego, who was once a hospital chaplain, believes that the ultimate solution will be to appoint an ombudsman at every hospital.

"The ombudsman would deal with the needs of patients, doctors and nurses," says Kavanaugh. "He would act as a confidant to the dying and the grieving. He would be someone other than the usual hospital personnel, who could make it possible for people to talk. In a case where euthanasia might be considered, he would be a general catalytic agent who would enable discussion to occur, who would bring together all interested parties.

"The ombudsman would bring decency into dealing with all the issues. He would raise the issue of medical ethics when appropriate, and could invite a chaplain to participate in any discussions.

"An important requirement would be that the ombudsman would be on an equal status with doctors and hospital administrators. In other words, he could voice his frankest opinions to doctors without fear of repercussions."

Some hospitals already have ombudsmen. The American Hospital Association estimates that nearly six hundred of the nation's six-thousand-plus hospitals have some form of patient representative program. Cedars of Lebanon Hospital in Los Angeles pioneered the concept back in the 1940s. Since then, other hospitals have created similar staff positions, with titles ranging from ombudsman to patient advocate to patient service coordinator.

"Hospitals can be an extremely dehumanizing place," says one ombudsman. "Every employee has a specific job to do, and often it seems no one has the time just to listen to what the patient and his family have to say. The doctors, the nurses, and the orderlies are so busy doing the countless number of things they must do that they may neglect the most important thing, which is the *human* needs of the patient. Ombudsmen can break through that terribly rigid hospital structure, and ensure that the patient as well as all other interested parties have someone sympathetic to discuss all issues and complaints with."

Euthanasia advocates also support the growth of "hospices," which are institutions to care for the needs of the dying, without the artificial aid of life-support systems. The most well-known hospice is St. Christopher's in London, which was opened in 1967. It is a human-oriented place, which honors the right of the patient to die peacefully while living as completely as possible during his last few weeks or months.

The family of the hospice patient is encouraged to continue being an important part of the patient's life, which invariably gives a psychological rejuvenation to the sick person. Family members actually "take over" from the staff, spending as much time at the institution as they desire. Visiting hours are freely abused, and families sometimes even stay overnight at the hospice.

There is also no age limit on visitors. Children of all ages are frequently seen playing in the rooms of their parents and grandparents.

The staff at St. Christopher's is also unique. It is intentionally large for a forty-four bed institution, leaving doctors, nurses, and even secretaries plenty of time to relate to the patients on both a medical and nonmedical basis. Unlike some hospitals, the staff of the hospice is encouraged to sit on a patient's bed, in order to touch and talk with him on a more intimate level. Embracing is a common practice.

The staff tries to give everyone the feeling of belonging to one large and loving family. In an article in the *Union Seminary Quarterly Review* (Winter 1972), Dr. Robert E. Neale relates how one patient described his first day at St. Christopher's. Wrote Dr. Neale, "Mr. D. said to me: 'When I came here in the ambulance, a doctor and a nurse were right there. Usually when I enter a hospital, they ask me my name, age, and so forth. You know what they said here? "Hello, Mr. D., welcome to St. Christopher's." I felt at home before I entered the building!' There is always time for staff to go outside the building to greet a patient. Once inside, very rarely is a patient passed by because a member of the staff is too busy."

Very little mechanical apparatus is ever used at St. Christopher's. Nasal tubes and intravenous feedings are never prescribed, so if a patient has difficulty in eating and swallowing, he is hand-fed by a staff member, even if this process takes several hours a day.

The patient makes most of the decisions in regard to his own care and treatment. Most of the medication is prescribed simply to keep the patient comfortable, free from the burden of pain and nausea. The purpose of the hospice is not to cure, but to make dying a more comfortable and humane process.

"The hospice is really a place where people can go and stay, and not be kept alive unduly," says Elizabeth T. Halsey of the Euthanasia Educational Fund. "I think it's definitely a thing of the future. But one of the problems is that the hospice will be an expensive proposition, much like nursing homes and retirement homes."

There are currently preparations being made for a hospice to be built in the suburbs of New Haven, Connecticut. Present plans are for it to be operating by late 1974, but $3 million will have to be raised by then to finance the construction of the new facility. It will have space for seventy terminally ill patients, plus furnishing out-patient care for seventy others who are able to live at home. The estimated cost for care inside the hospice will average 69 percent of the cost of a normal hospital's room rate.

"There is really no place in the general hospital for a dying patient," says Dr. Ira Goldenberg, a professor of surgery at the Yale school of medicine and a member of the New Haven hospice steering committee. "The goal of the general hospital is to heal patients, to make them healthy so they can leave the hospital as soon as possible. But the dying patient is not going to be healed. The hospital staff sees him as just taking up space."

Another member of the hospice steering committee, Florence S. Wald of the Yale school of nursing, says that the hospice has the potential of making dying more meaningful. "Dying is part of the life process, and in that sense, it can have substantial meaning to the individual. It can be a peaceful time for the dying person, a time even of joy, with a lot of nostalgia and reminiscing with those close around him "

Dr. Cicely Saunders, medical director of St. Christopher's Hospice in London, has witnessed the worthwhileness of the hospice environment. In *Death and Dying* (1969), Dr. Saunders writes, "We have a photograph of a patient and his wife taken for their golden wedding anniversary only forty-eight hours before he died. Though he did not have the energy to smile, the picture shows his peacefulness and his feeling of closeness to his wife. I recall that when he came to [us] he was confused and did not recognize his wife or anything else. But after a short while with us, he was himself once more. When his wife visited they were as close as they had been at any time during their fifty years of marriage. It is very important to share this 'moment of truth' in whatever way one can. It is very important to say 'Good-bye.' Good-byes matter. We all give importance to saying 'Good-bye' when we go on a journey—how much more meaning 'Good-bye' has now. We can do a lot to create this sort of quiet togetherness for a couple by telling a patient that we can help him cope with the pain as it comes and letting him know in advance that the moment of death itself is quiet. Then he can, as far as possible, have this moment alone with a relative, shielded from the things that the staff can do something about. You cannot take away parting and its hardness, but you can help it."

Hospices could bring about a more humanistic approach to dying, like the one advocated by British physician S. L. Henderson Smith in a 1971 address to the Voluntary Euthanasia Society. "We need to take dying out of the seclusion with which our prejudices have surrounded it," said Dr. Smith. "Dying should be a simple matter, a natural matter as it was before the excessive sophistication of medical science made it necessary for most people to die three or four times over. As Alexander the Great said, 'I am dying with the help of too many physicians.'

"When will the day come when a cancer sufferer, an old and weary person dreading leaving home for an institutionalized terminal existence, will be able to say to me, 'Doctor, I want to die' in as ordinary a voice as he might say, 'I want to have my gastric ulcer operated on,' and, the formalities completed, I shall be empowered to accede to his request: 'Drink this, my friend, you will sleep and no one will waken you'?"

8. Is Euthanasia of Severely Deformed Infants Justified?

A baby boy, born prematurely at a Maryland hospital, was diagnosed by doctors as a mongoloid (Down's syndrome), doomed to a life of severe retardation. To complicate the situation, further tests revealed the child was suffering from duodenal atresia—an intestinal blockage that prohibited him from eating and drinking.

Upon discovering the intestinal defect, doctors immediately prepared for surgery. Such a condition can usually be corrected with only a nominal risk. The baby was kept nourished through intravenous feeding until parental permission was received for the operation—but it never came.

The parents decided that it would be unjust to impose the burden of a severely retarded infant upon themselves and their other children. They chose to let the baby die. The doctors sought a legal reversal of the parents' decision, but

141

they ceased to pursue it when they learned that the courts would undoubtedly support the right of the parents to make the final judgment.

Incidents like this one, in which a severely retarded or crippled infant is allowed to die, have always aroused a loud public outcry. Because of the lifetime ahead of it, and because the baby has no voice in whether it will live or die, even the staunchest supporters of euthanasia are often silent when the case involves a child.

The Euthanasia Educational Fund in New York has never advocated that a child's life be ended by euthanasia. Most legislation that has been proposed over the years has not applied to persons under twenty-one.

The case in Maryland has drawn varied reactions from politicians, clerics, and doctors. At a 1971 conference in Washington sponsored by the Joseph P. Kennedy, Jr., Foundation, a doctor who cared for the mongoloid child before it died told of several other similar cases that had occurred over the previous five years. He said that difficult life-and-death decisions are made every week in hospitals throughout the country.

Another speaker at the conference, Harvard law professor Paul A. Freund, compared the dilemma of the parents and their retarded child to three mountain climbers, tied together as they ascend a mountain. If one falls, said Freund, the other two will realize that the only way to save themselves is to cut him free and let him die. Freund concluded that the parents, like the mountain climbers, made the right choice.

One doctor described the mental distress that the attending physicians in Maryland experienced while allowing the infant to die. They went to great extremes to disguise in their own minds what was really happening. In giving progress reports of the infant's starvation to the father, extensive medical terminology was used to make the reality of the situation appear as distant as possible.

The irony in so many mongoloid cases is that, were it not for intervention by medical science, most of these "abnormal" infants would die natural deaths shortly after birth anyway. Our society has now generally accepted the practice of allowing the fetus to be killed in utero if there is some indication that it might be born mentally or physically defective. But once the birth has occurred, doctors employ extraordinary methods to keep alive what may have been intended to die anyway.

A Southern California doctor wonders whether advances in medical science are always to the benefit of mankind. "Even just a century ago," he says, "the infant mortality rate was so high that mothers fully expected at least one-third of their children to die before reaching puberty. At that time, science had no cures for the major childhood diseases like smallpox and diphtheria.

"Thankfully, today, we have conquered most of the causes of infant mortality. However, at the same time, we can keep alive indefinitely severely deformed children whose lives are, for all practical purposes, worthless. Just as we look back in horror at the millions of youngsters who died of childhood diseases centuries ago, we must also feel the same type of horror for uselessly keeping alive the congenitally malformed children of today."

About one in six hundred births in the United States is a baby born with mongolism. Geneticists have discovered that mongoloids have forty-seven chromosomes inside their cell nucleus, rather than the normal forty-six, but there is no explanation of why this happens. The mongoloids who survive childbirth are impaired by tragic defects like severe retardation, blocked intestines, and congenital heart disease. Mongoloids who live frequently face a life without meaning.

A British hospital official, W. L. Dingley of the Association of Hospital Management Committees, once told a royal commission that keeping such infants alive is futile both to the infant and to his family. He said that when no hope exists for a mentally or physically abnormal baby, it should be possible for the infant to be put to death.

But most doctors refuse to even consider such a suggestion, relying on the moral reasoning that they cannot "play God." This, despite the fact they they "play God" in many other facets of their practice. As Dr. Alan F. Guttmacher wrote in an essay in the volume *Family Planning and Population Programs* (1966), "When it comes to many of the social problems of medicine . . . sterilization, therapeutic abortion, donor artificial insemination, and withholding resuscitative techniques to seriously malformed infants in the delivery room—doctors retreat behind the cliché that they 'won't play God.' This type of intellectual cowardice, this mental retreat is irrational . . . because through the nature of his work a doctor is constantly intruding himself into the work of the Diety. Does he wait for God to show his decision by making some outward manifestation before he undertakes a Caesarean section, orders a transfusion, or performs a risk-fraught open-heart operation?"

Some doctors, though, are acting differently from the norm. In the United States, there are now surgeons who refuse to operate on mongoloid children. They say they sense only future misery for the family of a mongoloid child. One doctor says he is especially annoyed by parents who plead that "everything possible be done to keep my baby alive," and who then subsequently place the infant in an institution where they never have anything to do with him again.

144

Recently in Los Angeles, a doctor chose to let an infant with serious birth defects die. The doctor, on his own, withdrew food from the baby after determining it had serious brain damage, a double cleft palate and lip, was probably blind, and had only stubs for arms.

The infant was not fed for two days. But on the third day, another doctor in the hospital overruled the decision by the first physician. Feeding was reinstituted and the baby is still alive today.

The physician who ordered that the baby's feedings be suspended said, "Some doctors believe that a 100 percent effort must be made on all babies to sustain life. To me, this is reasonable, but it's a copout. It doesn't take into consideration the circumstances that surround a baby's life. The mother has had a very tough time in life. She's unwed. She has three children at home. She said, 'How can I help this baby through a tough life with all these defects laid on him?' "

The doctor explained that "if she had showed some concern, some willingness to care for the baby," his decision might have been different. He also admitted that the choice was a difficult one to make—probably too much responsibility to place upon one physician.

To relieve doctors of some of this responsibility, there have been suggestions that the courts appoint adult advocates or defenders to represent the rights of newborn children. At the Kennedy Foundation symposium in Washington, Mrs. Sidney Callahan suggested that such an advocate should be unrelated to the parents, and should serve as a witness of the child's welfare. Mrs. Callahan, a psychologist, said, "A child ombudsman advocate could represent the community's commitment to the child; a witness to show that children do not belong to parents nor to the state as a form of property. Perhaps pluralism of philosophies could be safeguarded by allowing parents to choose among qualified advocates, as they choose godparents, for instance. But unlike the parent, pediatrician, priest, teacher, social worker, or judge, the child's defender would serve no other vested interest, but only represent the child from the child's point of view.

"Surely, in most cases parents fulfill their function of protection, but in the exceptional cases, or in a crisis, who protects the helpless powerless child? No child should be solely and secretly at the mercy of two adults or any professional in their service without some third party representing the child on behalf of the human community."

Mrs. Callahan believes that parents are often inappropriate parties to make the life-and-death decisions. "Surely parents are the last persons who should be granted the power to decide on the death of a newborn child. Demands of a dependent child are so great upon the parents and such deep emotions are aroused in parent-child interactions, that self-interest, hostility, and anxiety can be as present as protective love."

However, until an advocate system can be devised, any decision not to keep a severely deformed baby alive will usually be made jointly by parents and doctors. One recent instance involved a woman in her late thirties, who gave premature birth to a mongoloid infant. The chances of mongolism increase with the age of the mother, and doctors agreed on the diagnosis of mongolism immediately after delivery. For the first two days, the parents asked the normal questions for such a situation—"Isn't there any chance your diagnosis is wrong, doctor?" or "Why did this happen to us?" They contemplated the pros and cons of placing the baby in an institution, or of raising it at home.

On its third day of life, the baby began vomiting formula and bile at every feeding. He had an intestinal blockage, and surgery was necessary. The parents, though, asked their doctor if the operation was really necessary—was it justifiable in the case of someone who would never have the opportunity of a meaningful existence?

After much discussion, the choice was made not to operate. The mother told her physician that if she had known beforehand that the baby would be mongoloid, she would have had an abortion. Why then, she asked, could she not allow her baby to die now? The doctor agreed that their decision was a correct one.

Bernard Bard, an education writer for the *New York Post,* wrote about his own personal anguish when his wife gave birth to a severely retarded infant son. In a controversial article in *Atlantic* (April 1968), he described his baby's condition the way his doctor related it to him:

"The ears were set back too far on the head. The hands and feet were stubbier than normal. There was an in-turning of the final joint of the pinky fingers. There was a fold over each eyelid. There was a scruff of fat at the back of the neck. The hands and feet flexed back too far under pressure, but did not reflex. . . . And the tongue was too large for the mouth. . . . Few such children [according to the doctor] live beyond the teens. Those that do survive into adulthood are incapable of reproduction. The outlook for 'normal' mental development was about nil, he said, and only fifty-fifty that the child would be able to care for his own bodily functions, and not much more."

After receiving the depressing diagnosis, Bard then began to hear stories from neighbors about similar tragedies in other families. There was the woman who cared for her mongoloid son at home. At age fifteen, the boy was still wearing diapers, and his mother had sustained three miscarriages from lifting him. Another mother, who also cared for a mongoloid son at home, said that she wanted to outlive her boy by one day, just so she could experience a single day of freedom.

After much soul-searching, Bard decided to place his son in a sanitarium. He asked the institution's director not to use any life-prolonging treatment on the boy, such as innoculations for childhood diseases or oxygen if needed. Only a few days after the infant arrived at the institution, he died of heart failure and jaundice.

In retrospect, Bard wrote, "I believe that it is time for a sane and civilized and humane approach to euthanasia.

"I do not know how it should be practiced, or what committee should have a voice in the decisions, or what pill or injection might best be employed. I do know that there are thousands of children on this earth who should never have been born. Their lives are a blank. They do not play; they do not read; they do not grow; they do not live or love. Their life is without meaning to themselves, and an agony to their families."

The parents of many mongoloids and other seriously deformed children realize at some point how futile their child's life is. Distraught families place most of these afflicted children in a private institution, at an average cost of $500 a month, or in a state institution, supported by the taxpayers.

Some parents care for their defective youngsters at home. But the burden, physical and psychological, is wearing on both the parents and other youngsters in the family. One mother recalls the despair surrounding her severely retarded son. "There were really no problems in the first few months of Tommy's life," she explains. "But as he got older, his mental age really never advanced beyond about eight months. He began to do things that endangered his very safety, and he had to be watched every minute of the day.

"I remember one time when Tommy was six, I found him

trying to eat a rug in the bathroom," she says. "He would also climb out of his crib and balance himself on the edge of it. And he wouldn't learn. He would touch a hot oven, and then do it again and again because he wasn't able to comprehend its danger like a normal child can.

"Our whole family was affected. We wouldn't go anywhere—like on vacations or even on a Sunday outing—because of Tommy. We never went out to dinner. Tommy's brothers and sisters loved him, but they began to resent how he was holding everyone else down. I became so distraught that I eventually had a nervous breakdown."

When the burden seems too overpowering, and without legal euthanasia as one of their alternatives, parents are sometimes driven to other measures—often with tragic results.

Consider the case of Susan Coipel Vandeput, a twenty-four-year-old ex-secretary, who gave birth to her first baby in Liège, Belgium. After delivery, Mme. Vandeput told the baby's grandmother, "I hope they don't forget to put on her identity bracelet." Although she was not told immediately, it was not likely that Mme. Vandeput's baby would be confused with any other one in the hospital that week. Like thousands of other pregnant women back in the early 1960s, she had taken thalidomide. Her little girl was born without arms and with only winglike fingers. The baby's face was deformed and her anal canal emptied through her vagina.

Shortly after Mme. Vandeput was finally told about her baby's condition, she and the infant's grandmother decided that the child had no meaningful future. "We cannot let it live," she cried, "for its sake and mine."

On the day she and the infant left the hospital, Mme. Vandeput placed a lethal dose of sedative in a bottle, and fed it to the baby. By the following morning, the child was dead.

Shortly thereafter, Susan Vandeput was arrested and

149

charged with infanticide. The identical charge was filed against her husband, her mother, and her sister—all of whom were indicted as accomplices. The doctor who prescribed the sedative was also arrested.

In the courtroom proceedings, Mme. Vandeput admitted to the mercy killing, but justified it by saying it was better than letting the infant live. "I know I could not let a baby live like that," she said. "If only she had been mentally abnormal, she would not have known her fate. But she had a normal brain. She would have known. I would have had remorse all my life. There was nothing else I could have done."

When asked why she didn't consider placing the child in an institution, Mme. Vandeput replied. "That would have been a solution for me, but not for my baby."

The doctor who prescribed the sedative showed no remorse for what he had done. He told the court that he had realized the risk of prosecution, "But I thought about the moral and physical future facing the baby. I found it atrocious. I gave them the prescription. I do not regret it."

Public sentiment strongly supported the defendants. Radio Luxembourg asked its audience to respond to the question "Would you condemn the Liège mother?" There were over 17,000 replies, and 95 percent favored acquitting Mme. Vandeput. At the same time, a nationwide public opinion poll in England showed that more than two-thirds of the people favored legalizing euthanasia.

At the end of the six-day Liège trial, it took the jury less than two hours to acquit all the defendants.

Similar cases have occurred in recent years. In England, a major in the Royal Corps of Signals placed his three-month-old mongoloid son on a cot in the kitchen. He took a flexible gas pipe, put it on the baby's pillow, and then proceeded to turn on the gas. Within a few minutes, the infant was dead.

The father, forty-year-old Ernest Johnson, was brought to trial, and he told the court he had loved his infant son as much as his two older boys. But he was crushed by the doctor's diagnosis that the baby would never lead a normal life, would have no chance of earning a living, and could not hope to accomplish tasks more difficult than feeding himself. The doctor's words of "There is no hope" echoed in the father's ears until he finally took his son's life.

The court found Johnson innocent of murder but guilty of manslaughter. However, he was given the lightest sentence under the law: twelve months imprisonment. As the sentence was imposed, the judge told the grieving father, "No thinking person could feel other than the greatest sympathy for you. I accept that your terrible deed was done . . . solely to put your child out of its misery."

In an American decision, a father who mercifully killed his terribly deformed child was charged with manslaughter in the first degree. A jury convicted him of second-degree manslaughter but asked "for the utmost clemency." The defendant was sentenced to from five to ten years imprisonment, but the judge stayed the sentence and granted him probation.

In another tragic case in the winter of 1971, a thirty-five-year-old father drove his severely retarded six-year-old son to a secluded river, kissed the boy, and drowned him. The father then went to a nearby police station, and told the authorities what he had done. He said he had decided his son was better off dead, because during the boy's entire life, he was "just a living cabbage."

When the case was decided in court, the father was set free and placed on a year's probation. The judge said, "I am taking an exceptional course in an exceptional case." The court's decision may have been influenced by a petition urging clemency, signed by six hundred neighbors of the father who had seen the anguish the family had endured raising the child.

Joseph Fletcher, a teacher of Christian ethics at the Episcopal Theological School in Cambridge, Massachusetts, has called for some realistic legal guidance so distraught parents will not be driven to such drastic actions. He has suggested that the American Law Institute consider some changes in our laws about "elective death." In an article in *Atlantic* (April 1968), he said that there is really only a technical difference between a preventive abortion on a mentally or physically deformed fetus ("fetal euthanasia") and taking the life of a deformed infant after birth.

"To have given birth innocently to a Down's case," wrote Fletcher, "when we would not have done so if we had known the truth, does not of itself justify our extending the tragedy. By stubbornly persisting we only compound the evil; we make ourselves 'accessories' after the fact of a monstrous accident. We cannot be blamed for what we did not know, but we can be blamed when we do know.

"The only difference between the fetus and the infant is that the infant breathes with its lungs. Does this make any significant difference morally or from the point of view of values? Surely not. Life and human *being* is a process, not an event; a continuum, not an episode. It is purely superstitious to assert that life 'occurs' at fertilization or nidation or embryonic formation or fetal animation (movement) or birth or at school or voting age.

"To be a human is to be self-aware, consciously related to others, capable of rationality in a measure at least sufficient to support some initiative. When these things are absent, or cannot ever come to be, there is neither a potential nor an actual person. To be a person is a lot more than just to be alive."

Fletcher contends that, when considering the fate of a mongoloid, the welfare of the rest of the family must be weighed, too. "There is far more reason for real guilt in keeping alive a Down's or other kind of idiot, out of a false idea of obligation or duty, while at the same time feeling no obligation at all to save that money and emotion for a living, learning child. The learning child might be a retarded one with a viable potential, or just an orphan in need of adoption.

"To 'feel' obligated to prolong 'life' in the Down's case while failing utterly to see or accept any responsibility in the promising child's case is moral confusion worse confounded. From a human or moral point of view it is irresponsible."

It is unfortunate that financial considerations should play any part in determining whether a severely defective infant should be kept alive or not. But in this era of rising medical costs and growing life expectancy, finances are likely to become an increasingly important factor. Even the most severely retarded individual can now sometimes be kept alive for as long as sixty years. Over that long a life span, the cost of keeping an institutionalized person alive is now estimated at between $200,000 and $400,000—with sharp increases in costs inevitable. It now costs American taxpayers more than $1.5 billion a year to care just for all the children with Down's syndrome.

Dr. Walter Sackett, a physician, Florida state legislator, and strong euthanasia advocate, says that the state seems doomed to continue bearing the financial burden of the severely retarded. "In Florida, there are now about 1,500 individuals who are classified as severely retarded," he explains. "These individuals will never progress further than the diaper stage. Most are permanently bedridden. Some have such severe brain damage that they can do nothing more than sit and drool. Many cannot even feed themselves.

"If these individuals live to be fifty or sixty years old, it is going to cost the state of Florida four to six billion dollars to care for these 1,500 individuals," says Dr. Sackett. "In previous generations, the severely retarded could never have survived as long as they can today."

Even with the current large expenditures, many state institutions cannot adequately care for their retarded patients. At the Kennedy Foundation symposium, one doctor spoke out about the bleak future of a severely retarded infant who is kept alive and placed in a state home. Dr. Robert Cooke, pediatrician-in-chief at Johns Hopkins Hospital, said that some institutions for the retarded spend less for their patients' food than a pet owner would pay to feed a cat. Although Dr. Cooke joined a committee more than fifteen years ago to bring about changes in these institutions, he admitted that there has been almost no improvement over that time.

Most of these state institutions are strictly custodial: there are no training programs of any kind. The limited number of attendants barely has time to deal with the patients' necessities, like bathing, feeding, and cleaning.

A staff member of an institution in Georgia says that up to sixty severely and profoundly mentally retarded patients share a single ward there. Most of the patients are not toilet-trained, and they simply use the floor as their urinal. There is no talking in the ward, because most of its residents cannot speak. But even the few that can talk rarely say a word, spending most of their time in their own isolated private world.

In the summer of 1971, a group of New York State legislators toured the Suffolk State School for the Mentally

Retarded on Long Island. After the visit, one lawmaker said, "I felt I was ready to cry . . ." Another admitted, "I had to turn away."

They found retarded patients of all ages, many of whom were incontinent. In the dayroom for adult men were twenty or thirty males, some sitting in pools of urine, most of them staring blankly at walls or ceilings. Some were wandering in circles completely naked. One, wearing only diapers, sat in a chair with a football helmet on his head to prevent him from hitting his head against the wall.

In the child's ward of Suffolk, the legislators saw twenty-six profoundly retarded youngsters, all lying nearly immobile on plastic mats on the dayroom floor. Their bodies were so severely underdeveloped that their emaciated arms and legs stuck out in various bizarre directions. Children of ages eight and nine were so small that they appeared to be only two or three.

The hospital was so understaffed that legislators were told of residents not being fed, of patients drinking water from toilet bowls, and of attendants assigned to care for up to forty helpless children each.

Dr. Sackett, as a member of the Florida legislature's State Institutions Committee, recently visited an institution for the retarded in his state. "My colleagues and I," recalls Dr. Sackett, "saw a young man of twenty-five, curled up on the floor with his eyes open wide, staring at the corner of the ceiling. Apparently he had been lying in this fashion for all of his twenty-five years. He was being fed through a gastrostomy tube. He did not respond to anything I did. I spoke his name loudly. I tapped sharply on his shoulder. He didn't move at all.

"As we stood there watching him, a nurse approached him holding a hypodermic syringe. I asked her what it was.

" 'An antibiotic,' she replied.

"I was a bit startled, and asked her what the antibiotic was being used for. She answered, 'Why, he has an infection, we can't let him die.'

"Someone in our group spoke up and said, 'Why not? Is the man really alive?' That man will probably live another twenty-five or thirty-five years, doing nothing more than staring at that corner."

Undoubtedly, society will have to soon face up to the issue of whether the severely defective should be encouraged to live. Should mongoloid infants be kept "alive" at all cost when it is determined they have no chance for a normal life? Or what about an infant born literally without a brain: If he should develop pneumonia which would cause death in a short amount of time, should he be left alone to die?

Not long ago, a woman gave birth to a badly malformed infant. During a prenatal examination, doctors had determined that there was something wrong with the fetus. When the baby emerged from its mother's womb, their worst fears were confirmed. The infant's arms and legs were underdeveloped and misplaced. Its head appeared to be only a mass of protoplasm, with normal facial features all but unrecognizable.

The doctor who delivered the baby decided that merciful euthanasia was in the best interest of both the infant and its family. He placed the baby in a receptacle with instructions not to aspirate it, and went with a death certificate in his hand to talk with the father. But despite his orders, a nurse aspirated the baby. It proceeded to live nearly ninety days, the normal life expectancy for such births. The family's medical bills reached exorbitant levels over the three-month period. The mother, who had demanded to see the baby, became hysterical and suffered severe mental shock. For months afterward, the doctor who had originally intended to let the baby die was called a "murderer" by some members of the hospital's obstetrical staff.

An Arizona physician recalls how he had to deal with a similar situation in his own family fifteen years ago. His wife gave birth to a severely malformed infant, and after discussions with many other doctors, the parents concluded that the child "would never amount to anything" because of irreparable damage to its internal organs. A decision was made not to prolong the infant's life, and it was allowed to die. Since then, the doctor has supported changes in the legal codes to allow such actions to be taken openly and without public or legal censure.

As one physician says, "This is the most difficult choice a doctor can ever make. Is life worth living, even in a sub-human state? I've seen families torn apart—drained financially, physically and emotionally—praying to find some hope in a hopeless situation. Many times, when the baby does die, the family seems almost relieved that both they and infant are finally freed of this terrible burden."

When the Voluntary Euthanasia Bill was debated in England's House of Lords in 1969, one of the session's most dramatic speeches was made by Lord Segal, who is a surgeon. He told a hushed house of his "first decision to mercy kill." He described how, forty years earlier, a young expectant mother was in her third day of labor, with the situation complicated because her baby's head was impacted in her pelvis. It was much too late to perform a Caesarean operation, and the choice soon came down to saving either the mother or the child. The hospital staff decided that the child should be sacrificed, and an operation was performed.

But unexpectedly and to everyone's horror, the terribly deformed infant began to cry. "The mother was coming out of her anesthetic and would want to see her baby," recalled

Lord Segal. "I did not have time for a long deliberation. It would have been dreadful for this young mother to see such a thing. I asked a nurse to keep adding a few more extra jugfuls of warm water to the bath and I immersed the baby's head first. There were six or seven student nurses there, I suppose they could have laid an accusation against me of wilful murder or at least of infanticide, but after their initial dismay they acquiesced in what was done."

Lord Segal said that if faced with the identical situation today, he would do the same thing.

Dr. Foster Kennedy, former head of Neurological Division of Bellevue Hospital in New York City, was one of the earliest public advocates of legalized euthanasia for infants born with hopeless brain damage. In 1942, he proposed that when a defective child has reached the age of five, his parents may apply for euthanasia for their child. The case would then be studied by a panel of medical doctors, and reviewed twice more at four-month intervals. If after all this deliberation the panel decides that the child has no hope of any meaningful life, then Dr. Kennedy recommended that the youngster should be released from the agony of living.

When Dr. Kennedy made his proposal more than three decades ago, it was judged by many people to be a preposterous recommendation. But as the harsh realities of severely defective children become better understood, such proposals could someday become law.

9. Facing Up to the Realities of Euthanasia

More than at any other time in history, euthanasia is now beginning to be discussed openly in both the printed and electronic media. The complex issues surrounding euthanasia are finally being aired, and the common fears are being debated and sometimes resolved.

One of the most prevalent public anxieties about euthanasia is the possibility that, if legalized, it could sometimes be administered based on an inaccurate diagnosis. What if euthanasia is performed on someone who was thought to be dying, but his illness was wrongly diagnosed? In San Diego, for example, a doctor recently refused to give a tracheotomy to a patient in intensive care because he was unable to detect any brain waves in the patient, indicating there was no trace of life. The doctor concluded that the patient was dead, and that no heroic lifesaving measures should be taken. However, another physician disagreed, and he performed the tracheotomy. The patient recovered, left the hospital after serveral days, and is now back at his job.

Dr. I. M. Rabinowitch, in an address to the Medical Undergraduates Society of McGill University, emphasized the point that doctors are not infallible, and that mistakes in diagnosis have been made. Dr. Rabinowitch should know. Eighteen years before his address, he had been diagnosed as having terminal cancer of the esophagus. But the prognosis was wrong, and as the McGill audience could see, Dr. Rabinowitch was still very much alive.

Advocates of euthanasia admit that there is always the risk of a mistake being made, but that the chances are remote. The rare possibility of a wrong diagnosis, they argue, should not paralyze society into doing nothing.

The common argument that a cure could be found overnight for a terminal disease has also been countered by euthanasia supporters. They frequently hear the contention that no case can ever be considered "hopeless," since there is always the chance that a "miracle" remedy will be discovered.

"There just aren't that many overnight miracle cures," says Elizabeth T. Halsey of the Euthanasia Educational Fund. "Most doctors know what kind of research is going on in their specific fields. They know how near a breakthrough is, or whether it's still going to be years before any real cure is possible.

"There will always be exceptions—people who were at death's door and are quite well today. But on the whole, the doctor knows if there's any chance of recovery. Those miracles don't come overnight. If you follow any of the research, you know it takes years for cures to be found—first with experiments on animals, then slowly working them into use on humans."

160

In *Morals and Medicine* (1954), Joseph Fletcher writes, ". . . by no stretch of the imagination, in a typical situation, can we foresee a discovery that will restore health to a life already running out. A patient dying of metastatic cancer may be considered already dead, though still breathing. In advanced cases, even if a cure were to be found, toxemia has in all likelihood damaged the tissues and organs fatally."

Many defenders of euthanasia feel that the public has been slow to accept it because of the memories of Nazi atrocities committed in World War II. Hitler had thousands of ill people killed under the false pretense of euthanasia. German doctors provided the state with the names of patients who had occupied hospital beds for five years or more. These lists were examined and those in "undesirable" categories were selected to be killed. About 275,000 people—most of them with diseases like advanced Parkinsonism, multiple sclerosis, and brain neoplasm—were done away with "for the good of society." It became a common occurrence for doctors to inject poison into the hearts of their "undesirable patients." These murders were in addition to the Nazi genocide committed against the Jews.

The actions of the Nazi doctors so outraged physicians throughout the world that a new code of medical ethics was written after the war by the World Medical Association, stressing the sanctity of human life. Consequently, the present campaigns for legalizing euthanasia emphasize a system of ethics, and a constant respect for each individual human being.

Yet opponents of euthanasia often refer to what they call the "wedge theory," claiming that any liberalization of the euthanasia laws could be the first step to Nazi-type atrocities. They argue that even the slightest loss of respect for the sanctity of life could eventually have tragic results. It may not be long, they argue, before euthanasia is extended to

161

eliminate the senile, the physically crippled, and others who may "be of no service to the nation."

But is the slope as slippery as these euthanasia opponents insist? Such arguments hold little credence when appropriate statistics are examined. Consider the murder rates in England in two significant years. In 1939, there were 156 murders reported. In 1947, shortly after a war in which thousands of men were trained and disciplined to kill, the number of murders was 171. The next year, 1948, the number dropped to 162. Thus, even the war, which condoned murder on a massive scale, did not reduce society's reverence for life outside the context of war itself.

The "wedge theory" has not proved applicable for other controversial measures, including the sterilization laws. When the first sterilization legislation was introduced, its opponents contended that it would eventually lead to the compulsory sterilization of anyone at the whim of the government. But nearly seventy years have passed since the first sterilization law was enacted in Indiana. And in most states that have such laws, they are rarely used at all. In fact, for the most part, their use has been increasingly confined to voluntary sterilization.

The "wedge theory," although valuable for argumentative purposes, must be viewed cautiously. It can be raised against any new proposal, making even the most reasonable idea seem perilous. Yet simply because appalling consequences can be imagined is no reason to reject every new proposal. We know that patriotism can lead to imperialism, or that discipline of children can lead to severe child-beating. All ideas can be carried too far. But a civilized society should be capable of putting limits on its ideas, not rejecting them all outright. Reasonable use of euthanasia should not be dis-

162

carded solely because of its shameful and twisted application by the Nazis.

"It's unfortunate that some people would consider what the Nazis did as a form of euthanasia," says Mrs. Halsey. "What the Euthanasia Educational Fund is talking about couldn't be farther from the Nazi atrocities. We're interested only in voluntary euthanasia—in other words, allowing someone to die who has a terminal illness and who does not wish to have his life needlessly prolonged. From the hundreds of letters that we receive each week, most people aren't thinking in the Nazi terms at all. Quite the opposite, they're only thinking in terms of what's humane."

Dr. K. H. Southall agrees with Mrs. Halsey that euthanasia must be dealt with more realistically. Writing in the *British Medical Journal* (August 9, 1968), Dr. Southall said, "Medical progress is keeping alive, or rather 'preventing from dying,' many for whom life holds out no prospects of a worthwhile existence, and large numbers who have reached an age and condition in which their only prospect is mental or physical suffering.

"Voluntary euthanasia is not, as has been stated by some people who ought to know better, 'getting rid of unwanted old people.' It is gently helping over the border those, and only those, who specifically ask for it. If this new advance were legalized it is certain that the great majority would rather 'stick it out,' but at the same time it would be an enormous relief to know that there was a way out if life became insupportable."

As Dr. Southall says, modern science has made death a more unpleasant and prolonged experience than it has ever been before. Although there has been great progress in conquering pain, it is by no means complete. Some severe pain—

often the type involved in terminal illnesses—is refractory to drugs. Combine the pain with the other symptoms that medicine cannot usually control—breathlessness, vomiting, urinary incontinence, and the inability to talk or swallow—and the last stages of life can become a living death.

This was the case with an elderly patient suffering from inoperable throat cancer. As the disease continued to weaken him, his pain increased and he found it increasingly difficult to swallow even liquids. When the cancer thrust into his windpipe and larynx, his breathing became strained and he had trouble talking. For months he lingered on, and drugs ceased to help his worsening pain. Time after time, he asked to be released from the bleak and agonizing future he faced. His doctor refused to grant his request.

The realities of such situations makes liberalization of the euthanasia laws seem like a most compassionate course of action. Public opinion may eventually force lawmakers to support such legislation. In a 1969 poll conducted in England by Mass Observation, Ltd., 51 percent of those questioned agreed that voluntary euthanasia should be legally available to people suffering from incurable and painful diseases.

A revision of the current statues might have altered the treatment given in a Canadian hospital recently. In that case, the heart of a fifty-four-year-old man was restarted after he was struck by a severe heart attack. Although doctors were able to save his life, his central nervous system had been irreparably damaged. He lay in a coma, attached to machines that kept him breathing and nourished. All this was done with the full knowledge that his impairments were permanent, and that his capacity for a return to meaningful life was gone.

Life-sustaining measures seemed just as futile for an eighty-nine-year-old woman suffering from Paget's disease—an incurable bone ailment. Her plight was featured on the front page of a London newspaper, which described her as having little realization of being alive. She was saved from "certain death" twenty times as doctors rushed oxygen, intravenous injections, and drugs to her bedside. Her daughter, a woman of fifty-seven, pleaded unsuccessfully with the hospital staff to let the old woman die.

Doctors, feeling bound by both moral and legal considerations, usually refuse to permit euthanasia. But there are some who have different feelings. Dr. Rudolf Toch of the Pediatric Tumor Clinic at Massachusetts General Hospital sees no usefulness in needlessly prolonging the life of even small children. In an article in *Clinical Pediatrics* (July 1964), Dr. Toch wrote, "I will fight for every day if I have even the slightest chance of doing something more than just gaining one more day. . . . On the other hand, I recall a youngster whom we recently had on the ward with osteogenic sarcoma [bone cancer], the lungs completely riddled with tumor, who had not responded at all to the most potent chemotherapy and for whom we really had nothing further to offer. I did not feel any compunction at all about not doing thoracenteses, keeping intravenous therapy going, etc. All we did was give her adequate sedation, and I think she rather peacefully slept away."

Another doctor, appearing anonymously on a London television show, admitted to letting two patients die because "death was more merciful than life." One case involved a deformed baby—"a complete monster, I just put it to one side and left it unattended with inevitable results." The second instance, he said, occurred back in World War II, with a young boy who had his intestinal organs torn away by a bombing raid. The boy remained conscious, but "without the slightest hesitation, I gave him a heavy dose of morphine."

In another case, doctors encouraged the family of a thirty-four-year-old woman to let her die after serum hepatitis had caused irreparable brain damage. "The doctors told us that she would never recover," said the sister of the patient, "that her brain was all but dead. The whole family discussed it, and we decided that it was futile to keep a 'vegetable' alive. Only 'potential people' should be kept alive, and my sister no longer had any potential to function as a human being again.

"I think the doctors were very mature. One of them told us that life is more than a beating heart, that there is really no life if one is not able to enjoy it or to contribute something. I wish more doctors felt this way."

Sadly, it often takes a personal tragedy for some physicians to realize the intensity of suffering involved in watching a loved one die. This apparently occurred in 1969 to Dr. J. Thompson Stevens, a New Jersey physician well known for his treatment of cancer patients. His wife was dying of painful throat cancer, and after vainly searching for some legal release for her, he resorted to an illegal one. One evening the seventy-nine-year-old doctor used a gun to kill his wife, his forty-nine-year-old son, and then himself. In a one-page note he left for police, Dr. Stevens explained that his wife would have died soon anyway and that he himself was ill with emphysema. His son was a mongoloid, and once both he and his wife had died, there would be no family members left to care for him. Thus, wrote Dr. Stevens, while his wife was feeding his son in the upstairs bedroom, he killed them both. Police estimated that about seven hours later, the physician shot himself.

Staunch advocates of euthanasia believe that it is morally wrong for society to have placed Dr. Stevens in such a legal and moral dilemma. In his book, *The Sanctity of Life and the Criminal Law* (1957), Glanville Williams wrote, "It is good

166

that men should feel a horror of taking a human life, but in a rational judgment the quality of the life must be considered. The absolute interdiction of suicide and euthanasia involves the impossible assertion that every life, no matter what its quality or circumstances, is worth living and obligatory to be lived. The assertion of the value of mere existence, in the absence of all the activities that give meaning to life, and in face of the disintegration of personality that so often follows from prolonged agony, will not stand scrutiny. On any rationally accepted philosophy there is no ethical value in living any sort of life: the only life that is worth living is the good life."

10. Some Final Thoughts

Modern medicine has given man a dramatically increased control over death. But our legal statutes do not appear to have kept pace with the scientific advances.

We have the legal right to regulate most facets of our lives—except determining when our lives shall end. The law permits us—through a written will—to decide what will be done with our material possessions after we die. But it does not allow us any voice in what the fate of our own bodies will be if we are struck by a painful and incurable disease.

No state legislature has come even close to legalizing the right of a person to control his own final destiny. For at least the present, a patient still cannot authorize a doctor to let him die a dignified death if he should be struck by a fatal ailment.

Chief Justice Warren Burger has said, "The law always lags behind the most advanced thinking in every area. It must wait until the theologians and the moral leaders and events have created some common ground, some consensus." After all, it took some time for an acceptance of birth control, which is still far from being universally approved. The anti-abortion laws, too, were slow in falling.

But decisions of life and death can and should be made by individuals. Birth and death should not be viewed as processes to be accepted unquestioningly. The antieuthanasia laws now appear to be the next target of those who believe that man should be able to determine the circumstances of his own existence.

"I think one of the biggest problems is one of semantics," says Dr. Walter C. Alvarez. "So often the words 'euthanasia' and 'mercy killing' are used interchangeably. And 'mercy killing' is a very loaded, explosive term. Some people think that 'mercy killing' means doctors actually killing patients. I can't remember when a doctor actually ever killed a patient. I've heard of children born with tremendous deformities of the brain and skull, and doctors in such cases not making tremendous efforts to keep the infants alive. But that's certainly not murder. The term 'mercy killing' is a misnomer."

But no matter what terminology is used, a growing number of doctors are beginning to challenge the validity of using artificial means to keep hopelessly ill patients alive. Yet until the laws are changed to give all doctors and patients the freedom to choose among all the alternatives, the tragedies in hospital wards and nursing homes will continue.

"My grandfather deserves the right to die," says a thirty-five-year-old woman from Southern California's Orange County. "He's literally been nothing more than a vegetable for nine years. He's eighty-eight years old now and has had illness after illness. He's been so doped up for so long, he probably doesn't realize who he is, much less where he is.

"Just watching him and all his other relatives suffer so has made me an advocate of euthanasia. If there was a legal way for him to die peacefully, I'd support it. It shouldn't be a crime to let him die; the real crime is keeping him alive."

A young woman being treated by a sympathetic doctor recently chose a voluntary passive euthanasia when surgery revealed she had a rapidly spreading brain tumor. Her husband, in a conference with a chaplain and the physician, was told that further surgery would serve no useful purpose. The doctor, in fact, related a personal experience involving his own wife, who also had a spreading brain tumor that repeated surgeries had not halted. His wife, the doctor said, was still alive but was a vegetable. He advised the young couple—who had been married only three months—to go home and try to enjoy their last days together. They did. A month later she was dead.

Without a compassionate doctor, the young woman might have lingered hopelessly in the hospital for months—in both physical and mental anguish. The Euthanasia Educational Fund is trying to relieve that heavy moral and legal burden from doctors by providing the "living will" so patients can voluntarily choose to avoid a lingering death. "We would like to see some legislation," says Elizabeth Halsey of the fund, "where doctors wouldn't be afraid of malpractice suits if they allowed a patient to die. Doctors should even be able to give a patient a bottle of pills, and let the patient decide what his own fate will be. An overdose of the pills would be fatal."

The thought of euthanasia may be a disturbing one to those who have had no exposure to the horror of watching someone suffer through an incurable and painful death. But by the bedside of a hopelessly ill loved one, euthanasia sometimes seems like the most humane of all the alternatives.

The dignity of modern man is being assaulted from all directions, but probably the greatest onslaught occurs during the process of dying. How can an old man, in the last stages of a terminal disease, feel any sense of peace and dignity when he is relegated to die amid the impersonal confusion of a hospital, with tubes and machines hooked up to all parts of his body? No wonder some people are choosing to die at home, where they can feel a sense of security and be around those they love in their waning hours. And no wonder so many are investigating the merits of the living will, which would allow a person to die as he wishes. For to die with dignity is a basic right that everyone should have.

Man is entitled to a voice in determining both the quality of his life and the means of his death. An old woman expressed the feelings of many while suffering through the second year of an incurable cancer. "There are so many moments when I wish the end were already here," she told a hospital chaplain. "At age eighty-nine, sometimes I think I should have the right to die peacefully."